Edinburgh Introductions
Introductions to Scottish Culture

Adam Ferguson

Adam Ferguson

David Allan

Edinburgh Introductions
in association with
Edinburgh University Press

Edinburgh Review, 22A Buccleuch Place, Edinburgh
in association with
Edinburgh University Press Ltd.
22 George Square, Edinburgh.

A CIP record for this book is available
from the British Library

ISBN 1859332269

Printed and bound by CPI Antony Rowe, Eastbourne

Contents

.

Acknowledgements

I am grateful to a number of friends and colleagues for their assistance during the preparation of this study.

Several read substantial sections of my draft text. In particular, I thank David Spadafora, Nicholas Phillipson and Frank Muller, as well as that most intelligent of intelligent lay readers, Helena Thorley.

Although it is not unknown for an author to express gratitude to former students, in this case the debt is only too real. Successive groups at the University of St Andrews who have taken my Special Subject on the Scottish Enlightenment or my Honours Option on the historians of the eighteenth century would recognise much of the material and many of the explanatory ploys that follow. Without this substantial prior experience of having to present Adam Ferguson and his ideas to newcomers, it is difficult to imagine this book having been born.

No less is my work indebted to Ron Turnbull for his encouragment throughout the process of preparing this study, as well as for his perceptive advice in the latter stages, whilst I am also grateful to Cairns Craig and Alex Broadie for their helpful comments on my emerging text.

Chronological Table

1723   Born at Logierait (20 June)
1732–8 Attends Perth Grammar School
1738–42 At University of St Andrews (MA, 4 May, 1742)
1742   Enters Edinburgh divinity class
1745   Deputy chaplain to 43rd Highland Regiment, the Black Watch; ordination in Church of Scotland (2 July); Jacobite rebellion begins in Highlands (19 August)
1746   Promoted chaplain; present at assault on coast of Brittany; publishes *A Sermon Preached in the Ersh Language.*
1746–54 Service in Ireland, England and Flanders
1754   Abandons chaplaincy; visits Holland and Germany as private tutor to 'Mr Gordon'
1756   Outbreak of Seven Years' War; publishes *Reflections Previous to the Establishment of a Militia*; involved in the *Douglas* affair
1757   Appointed Keeper of Advocates' Library (8 January); resigns military commission (October). Publishes *The Morality of Stage Plays Considered*
1758–9 Resigns Keepership; tutor to sons of Earl of Bute in England
1759   Appointed professor of natural philosophy at University of Edinburgh (4 July)
1761   Issues *The History of the Proceedings in the Case of Margaret, commonly called Peg*
1761–3 Earl of Bute prime minister
1764   Appointed professor of moral philosophy at Edinburgh (16 May)
1766   Marries Katharine Burnet (2 October)
1767   Publishes *Essay on the History of Civil Society*
1769   Publishes *Institutes of Moral Philosophy*
1774–5 Tutor to Earl of Chesterfield on European grand tour
1776   Publishes *Remarks on a Pamphlet lately Published by Dr Price* (Mar.); American Declaration of Independence (4 July)
1778   Participates in unsuccessful Carlile Commission to America (17 April-19 December)
1780–1 Paralytic attack (December-January)
1783   Publishes *The History of the Progress and Termination of the Roman Republic*
1785   Retires from active teaching (14 May); becomes nominal professor of mathematics
1789   French Revolution
1792   Publishes *Principles of Moral and Political Science*
1793–4 Visits Germany and Italy
1795   Widowed (23 March)
1816   Dies in St Andrews (22 February)

Abbreviations

Chapter One

'From Infancy To Manhood':
Life and Times

Adam Ferguson may well be the most intriguing, and is certainly among the most complex, of the great figures of eighteenth-century Scottish culture. Not only did he come from an old Perthshire family, his political outlook and social position very much the product of the distinctive religious disputes and constitutional crises which had scarred late seventeenth-century Scotland. He also managed to survive into the second decade of the nineteenth century, to experience and reflect upon a very different world created by the French Revolution, the industrial transformation of social and economic structures, and the cult of Romanticism. Ferguson's life, however, for all its uncommon length, could scarcely have been less linear. Continual financial anxieties, an insatiably inquiring intellect and a temperamental need for diversion and adventure, together with his extreme longevity, all helped make Ferguson's interests and experiences more varied than those of most other British or European authors of his era. Not surprisingly, this diversity also left its distinctive mark on the several decades of original thought and writing that Ferguson eventually produced, as well as in the nature of the subsequent influence that his ideas and arguments would turn out to enjoy. As a result, it is more than usually necessary that we should begin our study of the man and his work by taking full measure of a lengthy and colourful life.

i

Adam Ferguson entered the world on 20 June 1723, the youngest child of nine born to his father and namesake, the minister of Logierait, a small village beside the River Tay in that part of central Perthshire which forms the transitional zone between the Scottish Lowlands and the Highlands. In a number of details these initial circumstances were far from promising for a future friend of British prime ministers and universally-acknowledged giant of the European Enlightenment. His father was in fact an ordinary rural clergyman working in a very ordinary parish.

Atholl, the district in which Logierait is situated, was far removed from the glittering lights of Edinburgh that would shine so brightly as the eighteenth century progressed; and Ferguson was certainly not born into the affluent and sophisticated lairdly society of the East Lowlands which would produce most of the other leading contributors to Scotland's contemporary cultural awakening. Instead, with his father already fifty-one when his last child was born, Ferguson was raised amongst a thinly-spread population of farmers and agricultural workers for whom Gaelic was usually the ordinary language and among whom both educational and economic openings were severely limited.

Ferguson senior, himself sprung from a family long resident in the district, had at least attended the University of St Andrews, though having reputedly learned to speak any English—in this case, Lowland Scots—only shortly before leaving school. More importantly, Ferguson's father had developed in his own younger days a strict attachment to evangelical Calvinism. This was a religious commitment by no means commonplace in upland Perthshire (then largely given to episcopalianism, as well as having pockets of residual Catholicism) and which carried with it two crucial implications for the philosopher's career. First, early exposure to what even by the standards of the time were probably relatively high levels of paternal piety seems to have left a permanent impression: a story is told, for example, that Ferguson, as a student, was mortified to be asked by a professor to prepare snuff on the Sabbath because he knew that his father would strongly disapprove. Such reactions doubtless help explain why Ferguson—although, as we shall see, his relationship with the Church of Scotland was to undergo significant modification—always remained prone to an intense earnestness of the sort which Calvinism has so often imparted in Scotland. Certainly they lent an austerity to his moral judgments, and an unmistakable seriousness of purpose to his wider intellectual disposition, which have been too easily under-estimated by many of Ferguson's modern readers.

Second, and at least as important, his father's early religious choices ensured that Ferguson would be raised, and would always remain, a staunch supporter of the Revolution of 1688–90, the political upheaval by which James VII had been forfeited by the Scots Parliament—ostensibly on grounds of his incurable Catholicism and absolutist tendencies—and the suitably Protestant couple William and Mary, respectively the late king's nephew and his daughter, inserted in his place. This in turn meant that Ferguson's own prospects in life were from the outset tied to the fortunes of the newly-entrenched presbyterian system of church organisation which had been reinstated by law as a foundation of Scotland's ecclesiastical affairs in the aftermath of that same Revolution. It is this fact above all which explains the philosopher's unwavering attachment, like that of his father before him, to the much-mocked Hanoverian dynasty which, following the reign of Mary's childless sister Anne, succeeded in turn to the British thrones in 1714. It also entailed Ferguson's strenuous endorsement (though, as will become clear, never uncritically) of the Anglo-Scottish Treaty of Union (1707), which was instinctively seen by most Scots presbyterians in the eighteenth century as a necessary bulwark of Britain's Protestant liberties. Finally, but not least importantly in the period up to the 1760s, this background also determined Ferguson's resolute opposition to continuing attempts by the Jacobite supporters of James's exiled Catholic heirs, themselves particularly numerous in Perthshire, to overturn the constitutional and ecclesiastical settlements arrived at throughout Britain by 1690.

It was having already acquired these strong personal commitments to what was in the first decades of the eighteenth century still by no means an uncontested political and religious order that Ferguson, as a fifteen-year-old youth, won a competitive bursary and proceeded to matriculate at St Andrews in 1738. Having passed through the parish school at Logierait and then through Perth Grammar School, it is clear that Ferguson had already achieved notable prowess in Latin composition. Certainly he had been identified as a youth of particular academic promise. It is therefore disappointing that we know virtually nothing about his personal experiences as a student at St Andrews. We do know, however, that this was a comparatively mundane period in the history of the university: from being the leading academic institution in Scotland a century earlier, St Andrews was by the late 1730s clearly behind not only Edinburgh and Glasgow but even the two Aberdeen colleges in the modernity of its curriculum and the celebrity of its staff. We can safely assume, though, that Ferguson was subjected to the normal undergraduate syllabus of the day, comprising a mixture of traditional moral philosophy, metaphysics, Latin, natural philosophy and mathematics, all of this delivered by competent though not greatly distinguished teachers like Francis Pringle, Charles Gregory and David Young.

Graduating MA in May 1742, with a secure reputation as an outstanding scholar and, with as-yet-unforeseen consequences, also as a brilliant mathematician, it was not unexpected that Ferguson should then begin the divinity course at St Andrews, a decision which appeared to confirm his intention to follow his father into the presbyterian ministry. But within a matter of months a significant change of heart had apparently occurred: in fact, Ferguson soon transferred himself to the same course at the University of Edinburgh. How far this was only because of the vaguely claustrophobic prospect of remaining in the same small coastal town is now unclear. But the evidence that his arrival in Edinburgh was rapidly followed by Ferguson's enthusiastic immersion in the much more dynamic social and cultural *milieux* available to the capital's divinity students suggests that his move from St Andrews was actually motivated by rather more positive considerations. Above all, it strongly hints at Ferguson's convivial personality and enjoyment of good company—key features of his adult life and not unrelated, as we shall see, to aspects of his social philosophy. It also indicates a determination to pursue his education in the most lively and intellectually-invigorating environment then available to a young Scot.

ii

Whatever the cause, to these crucial two years after 1743 can be dated what turned out to be the most important and influential friendships of Ferguson's long adult life. For his contemporaries in Edinburgh included the key figures of the future "Moderate" party, that faction of culturally-sophisticated and liberal-minded young clergymen who would soon dominate the Church of Scotland and play such a major part in the brilliant flowering of thought and literature after the 1740s which has become known as the Scottish Enlightenment. One was William Robertson, in time *de facto* leader of the Moderates, eventually to become a great Principal of the University and lauded as one of the age's most innovative and highest-earning historical writers. Another was Hugh Blair, already a minister of Edinburgh's prestigous Canongate parish and later professor of rhetoric and belles lettres, who would emerge as among the most popular sermonisers in the English-speaking world as well as a dominant literary critic in late-eighteenth-century Scotland. John Home, first a parish clergyman at Athelstaneford in East Lothian and then a much-celebrated dramatist, was also among Ferguson's friends. So too was Alexander "Jupiter" Carlyle, subsequently minister of Inveresk near Edinburgh and finally, following the posthumous appearance of his outrageously indiscreet autobiography (which even the nonogenarian Ferguson, who had prudently warned his late friend's executors against publication, thankfully did not live to see), the unrivalled memorialist of the Moderates and their era.

Of this remarkable circle of aspiring clergymen, all of whom were themselves the sons of ministers, it should be underlined once again that Ferguson was the only one whose origins lay beyond the rapidly-developing urban-focussed landscape of the Lothians which have always formed Edinburgh's natural hinterland. Indeed, not only is it probable that on his first arrival he was largely a stranger to Scotland's capital city. He was also alone among his immediate friends in having extensive first-hand knowledge of the Highlands and of the country north of the Tay. Almost needless to say, he was in addition the only one of the group, which would soon become absolutely central to the intellectual life of Edinburgh and of Scotland, who was to any extent conversant with Gaelic—interestingly, a language in long-term decline as a spoken tongue but, by the time the eighteenth century was drawing to a close and Ferguson himself was securely established as one of Scotland's leading cultural figures, increasingly acknowledged as a key distinguishing feature of the country's unique identity and heritage. These clear differences of background and perspective, as we shall see, also go some way towards explaining important features of Ferguson's philosophical outlook which differed from those of his principal Scottish friends and associates.

During his years as a divinity student in Edinburgh, Ferguson's intellectual development certainly seems to have quickened, stimulated by the peculiar combination of secular and religious learning in which he and at least some of his fellow-students had become immersed. It bears repeating, however, that theirs was a relatively daring position for aspiring churchmen to adopt in Scotland in the early 1740s. Certainly it would have been considered downright provocative by some of their less adventurous contemporaries—little more than a generation after Thomas Aikenhead, another intellectually fashion-conscious Edinburgh undergraduate, had been hanged for alleged blasphemy. In particular, Ferguson and his associates seem to have been fascinated readers and budding disciples of a series of advanced lay thinkers. Chief among these was Anthony Ashley Cooper, 3rd Earl of Shaftesbury, the English nobleman who had insisted that humans possess an instinctive benevolence towards others. Another favourite of the emerging Moderates was Joseph

Addison, the English journalist and social commentator who had popularised Shaftesbury's ideas and vigorously promoted the active moral and cultural improvement of the modern British public through his stunningly-successful and much-emulated magazine *The Spectator* (1711–12). But most importantly in a Scottish context, Ferguson's clique were greatly affected by Francis Hutcheson, professor of moral philosophy at Glasgow (where Carlyle had also studied prior to coming to Edinburgh): indeed, Hutcheson's formalisation of these seductive doctrines, to the considerable annoyance of the Church of Scotland's more conservative clergy, had brought Shaftesbury's uplifting ideas about man's essential good nature and Addison's claims about the wide-ranging benefits of polite socialisation into the very core of the undergraduate curriculum.

It is difficult today for us fully to appreciate the subversive potential of a moral philosophy founded on the seemingly harmless optimism of Shaftesbury and Addison. But with the attachment of so many early eighteenth-century Scots to a rigid Calvinist orthodoxy—their zeal intensified by fears that the unexpected victory won by presbyterianism in 1690 might yet prove fleeting—the dangers perceived in the new secular ideas by many in Scotland's national church, and especially by many of Ferguson's older contemporaries, should not be underestimated. As recently as the 1720s John Simson, another Glasgow professor with a fondness for fashionable lay thinking, had faced concerted attempts by less broad-minded clerical colleagues to suppress his allegedly heteredox teachings: ultimately Simson had been relieved of his academic duties. And it was in 1727, actually within the Moderates' own lifetimes, that Scottish officialdom had incinerated its last witch, an unfortunate woman sent to her doom at Dornoch with the connivance of the sheriff of Sutherland. In such an atmosphere, instinctively suspicious of anything that might challenge the certainties of traditional Calvinism, it would clearly be unwise to make too much of our own retrospective knowledge that Ferguson and his friends not only escaped any serious punishment for their intellectual curiosity but would even go on to enjoy successful and well-rewarded careers as the leaders of their church. In the early 1740s they were in fact positioning themselves as the supporters of an *avant-garde* culture which was still, sometimes haltingly, often with understandable nervousness, in the process of asserting itself—especially in Scotland and among the country's previously hidebound presbyterian clergy.

It was at this point, after a period during which Ferguson's mind was being decisively oriented towards some of the most exciting secular ideas of the emerging Enlightenment, and with his life permanently brought into close convergence with other rising talents who would exercise great influence in Scotland in the coming decades, that another unexpected departure occurred. Rather than completing the Edinburgh divinity course and entering the parish ministry, as would certainly have happened in the ordinary course of things (and as his father had surely anticipated), Ferguson, despite having completed only half of the normal six years' preparation for ordination, accepted in 1745 a deputy-chaplaincy in the recently-established 43rd (later 42nd) Highland Regiment, the Black Watch—in the process ensuring that he would also be the only major thinker of the Scottish Enlightenment, and one of comparatively few in Europe as a whole, to have acquired substantial personal experience of professional soldiering. This opportunity, perhaps attractive because it combined the chance of early responsibility with the prospect of genuine adventure, had its roots, like so many eighteenth-century job openings, in Ferguson's proximity to well-placed patrons. Indeed, in this case it was the Duchess of Atholl, mother of the regiment's first colonel and representative of a great Perthshire dynasty which had earlier installed Ferguson's own father at Logierait, who had made his advancement possible. In fact, despite his obvious inexperience as a clergyman, Ferguson appears to have been specifically chosen by the duchess so as to provide her slightly-unpredictable son with a young companion of known reliability.

In the event, the arrangement proved a happy one for all concerned. Ordained by special dispensation of the church's General Assembly in July 1745, not least on account of his Gaelic fluency—still an unusual and much-prized skill among government-supporting presbyterian clergy—Ferguson would serve with his regiment in Flanders, England, Ireland and off the coast of Brittany through the latter part of the War of the Austrian Succession. Numerous tales of the chaplain's heroic soldiering on the field of battle, largely the product of wishful-thinking by the later admirers of a revered thinker and teacher, have long been disproved and can safely be discounted: in particular, though often-repeated, the story of his derring-do at Fontenoy in May 1745 is certainly apocryphal, since Ferguson was at that time still a divinity student in Edinburgh. We should be in no doubt, however, that, once with the Black Watch, Ferguson was a well-regarded minister to his flock: his promotion to full

chaplain after the first year's service confirms that he had been recognised by clerical and military colleagues alike as a competent minister
and an invaluable member of the regimental community.

It is also difficult, as we shall see in later chapters, not to try to discern the genesis of certain features of his later intellectual outlook in
these powerfully-formative experiences of soldierly life and deadly warfare acquired by Ferguson in the eighteenth-century British army. Above
all, the over-riding importance of duty, courage, loyalty, patriotism and
self-sacrifice, among the most recurrent themes in his philosophical and
historical writings many decades afterwards, was surely drummed into
the young clergyman by his own first-hand involvement in active military service. At the same time, it should be emphasised that his army
career was in no sense merely a transitory phase in Ferguson's life, as,
partly because of the limited information we have for his life during
these years, it has been made to seem in some biographical surveys—in
other words, a brief interruption amid an inevitable progress towards
literary fame and academic eminence. In fact, Ferguson spent almost
a decade in the Black Watch. We should therefore regard him at this
stage as a Hanoverian clergyman and military officer of growing force
and authority, whose earliest publication, once more facilitated by the
good offices of the Duchess of Atholl, appeared in 1746, an English
translation of a passionately eloquent Gaelic denunciation of Charles
Edward Stuart, France and Roman Catholicism. Indeed, in this notable
work Ferguson sought to reinforce as well as to vindicate the loyalties of
Highland soldiers whose allegiance to Church, government and crown
might otherwise have been open to question amid the last and most
disturbing of the Jacobite rebellions.

iii

Ferguson's evident success and popularity as a regimental chaplain did
not prevent him from arriving in 1754 at the next of several important
life-changing resolutions. For it was around this time that he determined
to leave the army, whilst simultaneously progressing towards the even
more momentous move of renouncing his clerical vocation: certainly,
we know that, on leave from his regiment and already travelling in the
Netherlands and in Saxony as a gentleman's tutor in October of that
year, he even wrote a letter from Groningen to Adam Smith, another of

his friends from Edinburgh days, in which he requested to be addressed 'without any clerical titles, for I am a downright layman' (C I:10). Much speculation has inevitably surrounded the origin of these decisions, given their apparent suddenness and their obvious importance for an understanding of his intellectual development. Hurt at not having been granted the Perthshire parish of Caputh in 1748 by the Duke of Atholl is one explanation commonly offered. Another is his failure to secure the more attractive living of Haddington in East Lothian, for which he was still applying unsuccessfully as late as 1756. But it seems more likely that the somewhat drawn-out process of leaving the Black Watch and abandoning the ministry, coming in the period following his father's death (which had occurred in July 1754) and in light of his intimacy with men who were now at the heart of Scotland's emerging liberal culture, should be understood as part of a more considered plan of action, forming gradually in Ferguson's mind over a period of several years. In fact, he appears to have decided that he needed to throw himself whole-heartedly into the "republic of letters", the international community of writers and thinkers which by the 1750s was steadily advancing the Enlightenment throughout Europe, and not least—a pleasant surprise to some—in Edinburgh itself.

Certainly the evidence of Ferguson's subsequent activities supports the view that he turned his back upon a clerical career in the mid-1750s not in an ill-considered fit of pique but because of a growing and ultimately irresistible yearning to establish himself, as a number of his closest friends were already doing, as an intellectual and man of letters. Initially he was forced to survive by a variety of expedients—including once again as the travelling companion and tutor to a prominent young gentleman, this time John Fletcher, son of Lord Milton, Scotland's Lord Justice Clerk and, as political agent for the 3rd Duke of Argyll, effectively the country's principal power-broker. In January 1757, however, Ferguson, with the help of his ever-increasing number of well-placed sponsors in Edinburgh, succeeded David Hume in the not very well-remunerated position of Keeper of the Advocates' Library, the city's most important scholarly and research facility. Early the next year, having formally disposed of his military chaplaincy (the delay in finally severing this tie reflecting not any lingering doubts but rather a lifelong dread of exposure to financial insecurity), Ferguson moved to Harrow in England to take up a tutorship to the sons of the Earl of Bute, who would emerge within two short years as Britain's first Scottish prime

minister: this would in time prove yet another beneficial personal connection for Ferguson.

These were also years during which Ferguson, despite the initial pre-
cariousness of his economic circumstances, was throwing himself energetically, along with his friends, into the cultural and political life of
Edinburgh. One *cause célébré* in which he inevitably became embroiled at
this time was the *Douglas* affair of 1756–7. This was a bitter controversy
among the presbyterian clergy (of which Ferguson was strictly speaking
a member for the remainder of his life) over his friend John Home's
composition of a play of that name and the willingness of his Moderate
associates to attend the Edinburgh theatre to support it. Ferguson actually assisted Home in the first staging of *Douglas*, including taking part
in a reading of the text. He subsequently published a short pamphlet,
The Morality of Stage-Plays Seriously Considered (1757), in which he
defended play-going in the face of vociferous attacks from conservative
and evangelical critics who regarded it not merely as intolerably frivolous
for a clergyman to patronise the theatre but even as tantamount to the
open encouragement of public immorality. And, having been personally
present at several performances of the drama, he was even forced to fend
off malicious charges along the same lines submitted to the Presbytery of
Edinburgh by more reactionary elements within the local clergy.

Ferguson's skill as a propagandist was also revealed in his central role
in the militia controversy. This arose during the late 1750s because of the
British government's refusal to allow the Scots, on the same basis as their
English partners, to recruit volunteer forces to defend the local coastline
against likely French invasion. The resulting debate rumbled on from
the time of the Seven Years' War until the government's final capitulation
on the issue in the 1790s. But through the intervening decades it always
provided a reliable focus for simmering anger among loyal Scottish
Britons at the lack of respect for them displayed by suspicious English
ministers who still appeared to think that any Scot bearing arms, at least
domestically, was secretly bent on raising yet another new Jacobite rising. As utterly reliable supporters of the Hanoverian order—several of
them, including Carlyle, Robertson and Home, had actually tried to
defend Edinburgh against the Jacobite rebels in 1745—the Moderates
understandably resented this unwarranted slur on their political loyalties. They also became adept at emphasising the moral as well as military
benefits which would accrue in Scotland if a militia, the ideal outlet
for the legitimate energies of active and public-spirited citizens such

as themselves, were at last to be raised. In December 1756 Ferguson's anonymous *Reflections Previous to the Establishment of a Militia* was published in London. Four years later, his amusing satire on the same subject, *History of the Proceedings in the Case of Margaret, Commonly called Peg...* (sometimes erroneously attributed to Hume), also appeared anonymously. And in the years ahead, particularly through the convivial vehicle of the Poker Club (established in 1762 to, as Ferguson supposedly put it, 'stir things up'), he would continue to pursue the militia cause with undimmed vigour.

The most celebrated controversy in which Ferguson became involved during his first decade back in Edinburgh, however, was certainly the Ossian affair. This had been provoked by the publication in 1761 by James Macpherson, an ambitious young scholar from Inverness-shire, of translations of a previously unknown Gaelic epic poem which he claimed to have recovered and successfully reconstructed. The original work, moreover, was held by the brash and boastful translator to be nothing less than the lost masterpiece of Ossian, a third-century Celtic bard who had apparently recorded in strikingly passionate and sentimental verse the extraordinary deeds of Fingal and other hitherto-obscure Caledonian heroes. The result, between Macpherson's inordinately proud Scottish defenders and loudly incredulous English critics like Dr Samuel Johnson (with embarrassed Edinburgh doubters like Hume triangulating with understandable delicacy between the two parties), was probably the most notorious and beyond question the most entertaining literary dispute of the century, with the text's historical authenticity, and thus its self-appointed translator's basic integrity, the main points at issue.

Given Ferguson's unique linguistic abilities among the leading Edinburgh men of letters, it is unsurprising that his Gaelic facility should have been invoked at an early stage in patriotic support of Macpherson's scholarship. But his role in defence of this key totem of Scottish cultural virility would lead as late as the 1780s to a particularly unpleasant literary quarrel, played out in the national newspapers, arising out of Ferguson's involvement in a visit to Edinburgh in 1765 by the distinguished English antiquarian Thomas Percy. This famous student of British literature had been persuaded of Ossian's veracity only when finally presented with a Gaelic-speaking undergraduate student who was apparently able to recite similar material drawn from out of the same genuine Highland oral tradition as Macpherson had purportedly used. Subsequently, however, Percy had formed the view—whether correctly

or not remains a matter of dispute—that he had merely been the victim
of an outrageous fraud deliberately engineered by Edinburgh's unscrupulous intelligentsia, with Ferguson allegedly among the principal con-
spirators.

Academic advancement had not, however, been long in coming to a
man who had successfully made himself such a central fixture in the cultural and intellectual life of Scotland's capital city. In July 1759, in what
had actually been only the last of several attempts to secure Ferguson a
professorial position befitting his undoubted talents, his friends, led by
Hume and Robertson and with the considerable additional weight of
Lord Milton not particularly well-concealed in the background, eventually contrived to have the Town Council, which then controlled academic
appointments, elect him to the vacant chair of natural philosophy at the
University of Edinburgh. This decision must in many ways be regarded
as curious—perhaps even reckless, to our eyes—given Ferguson's conspicuous lack of relevant professional experience and the availability of
a much better-qualified rival applicant (rather illustrating the relatively
narrow social world in which Ferguson and Scotland's intelligentsia
moved, this was actually his own cousin and Edinburgh landlord, James
Russel). The appointment was, however, vindicated when, with wholly
characteristic single-mindedness, Ferguson immersed himself in his new
subject so as to compile a full course of lectures and experiments and set
about his teaching duties with such energy and aplomb that by 1762 the
student roll had been increased from nine to as many as eighty undergraduates.

As a teacher of what we should probably call "natural science",
Ferguson therefore made himself a remarkable success—in spite or perhaps because of his apparent limitations. In any case, his ability to master
a discipline with which he had only previously had academic contact as a
talented mathematics student at St Andrews twenty years earlier was certainly helped by the comparatively small distance which then separated
the study of the human and the natural worlds: as we shall see in due
course, the methods, the terminology, even the objectives, were often
the same. Moreover, the circles in which Ferguson had been operating
in Edinburgh since 1754 must have provided further encouragement
as he negotiated his way through an unfamiliar curriculum. Another
cousin was none other than Joseph Black, the great experimental scientist who would soon become famous for explaining the phenomenon of
latent heat and for isolating carbon dioxide: the two men actually lived

together, sharing Russel's house, during Ferguson's first years back in Edinburgh, and Ferguson would later write a warm biographical memoir of Black. James Hutton, an intimate of both men, was also at this very time beginning to develop the astounding theories about the formation of the planet, a foreshadowing of modern geology, which would be announced many years later in the path-breaking *Theory of the Earth* (1785). And since June 1756 Ferguson had himself been a prominent member of the Select Society, the city's premier intellectual institution, in which students of man and society like Hume, Smith, Lord Kames and the Moderate clergymen mingled easily with pioneering investigators of the natural world such as the anatomist Alexander Monro and the chemist William Cullen—both of the latter also subsequently among Ferguson's professorial colleagues at the University.

Yet for all his success in making himself a more-than-adequate teacher of natural philosophy, there can be little doubt as to where the real focus of Ferguson's intellectual interests still lay. These had perhaps revealed themselves most tangibly in a thought-provoking draft "Treatise on Refinement" which in 1759 was circulated privately among his friends, including Hume—whose comments on Ferguson's ideas were at this stage still highly favourable. They had more lasting effect in 1764 when a vacancy arose in Edinburgh's prestigious chair of pneumatics and moral philosophy: applying immediately for a position which he had probably long coveted, Ferguson was, with the decisive support of Robertson, Bute and Milton, successfully translated later that same year, now past his fortieth birthday, to the professorial position for which his talents manifestly best suited him. Once again, his exceptional talent, but also the powerful backing of well-placed patrons, had secured a vital opportunity for Ferguson.

This new turning marked the beginning of perhaps the most productive few years in Ferguson's long life. In 1766 he married twenty-year-old Katherine Burnet, Black's niece, with whom he would eventually have seven children, the first born in 1768. And in 1767 his first and most enduringly-successful book, *An Essay on the History of Civil Society*, was finally published, a full-length study of the progressive evolution of human society which at once looked back to the draft "Treatise" out of which it had grown and forwards to Ferguson's assured status as a leading luminary of the mature European Enlightenment. For the *Essay* was identified almost immediately by his friends as a major work contributing to what Hume, just about the only one of Ferguson's circle to express anything other than unqualified admiration for the book, had in his *Treatise of Human Nature* (1739–40) grandly dubbed "the Science of Man" (THN xv). As we shall see, however, and as is perhaps especially the case with many of the landmark works of modern thought, the *Essay* was characterised less by complete originality than by a winning ability to bring together a number of different interests and arguments, many of them to some degree familiar from other contemporary or earlier writings, and to do so in a way which was not only particularly pleasing and persuasive in manner but also unusually coherent and thought-provoking in form.

iv

Underscored, as we shall see in Chapter 6, by the *Essay*'s favourable critical reception, by its translation into a number of foreign languages and by its subsequent re-appearance in successive new editions, Ferguson's intellectual reputation and professional position, always vital considerations for a surprisingly anxious man, were far more secure by the early 1770s. Building on the lecture notes produced on the strength of his new chair, in 1769 he also issued the *Institutes of Moral Philosophy*, which again managed to more than make up in popularity for what it actually lacked in novelty. Indeed, this publication, essentially a *précis* of Ferguson's course arranged under a series of headings, recalled in several respects the intellectual commitments to which he had first openly subscribed as an Edinburgh divinity student more than twenty years before: Shaftesbury and Hutcheson, as well as his friend Smith, were the chief modern sources for its increasingly uncontroversial moral principles, now widely acceptable to (and indeed among) the leading Scottish clergy. Like the *Essay*, and in certain quarters even more so, the *Institutes* were an immediate success on the international stage, firmly establishing Ferguson as a teacher able to convey his sense of the overriding importance of philosophically-grounded moral principles within a comprehensive and, perhaps above all else, a useful education.

Even this great professional success, however, seems not to have brought Ferguson the complete satisfaction and peace of mind that he appears always to have craved. As a skilful and well-regarded teacher, he had certainly increased the student intake at Edinburgh dramatically: the thirty-nine undergraduates taught moral philosophy in 1764 had within just two years become one hundred and thirteen. But private financial concerns, particularly after marriage and starting a family, together with the innate restlessness which rarely left him for long, still led Ferguson to seek other potentially lucrative outlets for his energies. Despite the respectable emoluments of an Edinburgh professor, he had always sought to enhance his earnings by taking on the private tutoring of well-to-do undergraduates: this he continued to do in spite of his growing eminence. But when his University income finally dipped after 1770 as an unavoidable consequence of a wider economic downturn in Scotland which badly affected the institution's overall recruitment, it was almost inevitable that Ferguson would look to combine his love of travel and his innumerable personal connections in pursuit of yet more new opportunities for well-paid diversion.

Much of the period between 1772 and 1774 was duly taken up with Ferguson's attempts, ultimately abortive, to get himself appointed to a commission of investigation which the East India Company was expected to despatch to the sub-Continent to review its employees' increasingly-notorious activities: typical of both his insatiable curiosity and his seemingly limitless range of useful contacts, Ferguson had already been ransacking the university library for information on India and had been in touch with his former student and friend John Macpherson, then in Madras and, after a spell as Hastings' successor as Governor-General, subsequently Sir John (or just plain "Johnny MacShuffle" to his many enemies). By late 1773, however, Ferguson had accepted yet another profitable position which would take him away from his family and his teaching duties in Edinburgh, this time as tutor to Philip Stanhope, 5th Earl of Chesterfield, an appointment which brought with it a substantial pension for life.

This latter opening itself proved double-edged. On the one hand it allowed Ferguson to lead his young charge on an extensive European tour, taking in Paris and Geneva, Italy and Germany, as well as visiting Voltaire himself at Ferney, an encounter about which he wrote memorably to Robertson. On the other, the Town Council of Edinburgh, ostensibly angered by their professor's employment of a mere substitute but perhaps also interested (as Hume alleged) in inserting a particularly well-favoured rival as his replacement, moved in April 1774 to declare his chair vacant, a decision which only the timely intervention of Ferguson's ever-willing friends and patrons, this time with Blair in the vanguard, would eventually see rescinded. Removed as the young man's tutor in

June 1775 when Chesterfield acquired new guardians, Ferguson shortly afterwards threw himself into the bitter controversy provoked by the recent outbreak of the American Revolution, towards which, as a natural friend of church and state, and as a personal friend and supporter of several of the king's chosen ministers, he adopted a distinctly hostile stance. In 1776, for example, he published at government expense *Remarks on a Pamphlet lately Published by Dr. Price*, an anonymous riposte to Richard Price, the Welsh dissenting minister whose open support for the rebel colonists had incensed establishmentarian opinion throughout Britain: a fascinating piece despite its somewhat forced circumstances, the *Remarks* rests upon Ferguson's insistence, not unrelated to his philosophical interest in the conditions in which human communities first arose, that 'men, by entering into society, give up a part of their Natural Liberty' (R 4). And between April and December 1778 Ferguson was himself in America, where he visited New York and Philadelphia as a member of the Carlisle Commission which unsuccessfully attempted to negotiate acceptable terms with Congress. By 1779, and clearly in recognition of his conspicuous services to the British government in this great hour of national crisis, Ferguson had been awarded an additional annual pension from the crown.

v

Politics, in which Ferguson had been implicated in various ways since his early connection with Lord Milton and his long-running infatuation with the militia question, were also an important diversion for him after his return from America. At the 1780 general election, he was much involved once again with the poet Macpherson, this time in a failed attempt by supporters of Lord North's government to unseat the opposition-minded incumbent George Dempster in the Perth Burghs: ironically, Dempster was one of Ferguson's most reliable supporters on the militia issue, but his decision to support American independence and to align himself with the government's opponents amid the continuing national crisis occasioned by the war counted very much against him at this time. More intriguing still during these years was Ferguson's own decided ambivalence towards the gathering movement for parliamentary and administrative reform in Britain. He was, of course, an instinctive conservative, and was predictably nervous about the threat to the social order which some of the more radical campaigners undoubtedly represented. But he was also simultaneously attracted by those aspects of the reform programme which held out the hope of eradicating the worst excesses of the existing electoral corruption which, as a moralist and political philosopher, he genuinely disliked.

His response to the French Revolution, when it came, was also very far from straightforward. Certainly Ferguson seems to have been much less concerned about domestic events in France than most other conservative observers in Scotland, who, like another of his eminent former pupils, Henry Dundas, Lord Advocate and a leading cabinet minister in London, genuinely feared that Britain would follow in the same direction if any kind of domestic reform were now attempted. Indeed, Ferguson, although naturally unwilling to support the wilder constitutional experiments of the French, and especially the attempts at social levelling which had rapidly descended into violence and mass murder, was fascinated, as we shall later see, by the creative political energies and renewed moral fervour which the Revolution had also seemingly unleashed among the citizenry—with its self-conscious resonances of the Roman republic in which Ferguson himself had long believed that some of the highest human ideals had successfully been harnessed.

The period leading up to the Revolution had also been one of illness and some significant changes in Ferguson's private life. A paralytic stroke suffered in December 1780 had led to a lengthy recuperation under Black's personal supervision: since this involved, amongst other things, Ferguson's permanent conversion to vegetarianism (a practice which Black already followed), this is the source of the delightful observation in Henry Cockburn's *Memorials* that Ferguson's son (later Sir Adam) could recall often having seen the two old philosophers together 'rioting over a boiled turnip' (MOT 50). It was also while taking the waters at Bath as part of his lengthy programme of recovery that Ferguson completed the draft of his long-awaited next book, *The History of the Progress and Termination of the Roman Republic*, begun many years earlier and finally published in 1783. Notwithstanding the longer-lasting fame of the *Essay*, it is worth noting that this was actually Ferguson's own favourite work—not least, as we shall find in Chapter 5, because of his fervent belief in the continuing relevance of the Roman republic's experience to modern British readers.

Over the next few years Ferguson's vigour was in many ways restored, even though in May 1785 he finally relinquished the chair of moral philosophy in favour of his distinguished former pupil Dugald Stewart. In its place, Ferguson took up the vacant professorship of mathematics—from which, this time by agreement with the Town Council, he drew a significant income and paid John Playfair, one of Hutton's younger associates, to act as his substitute. In practice, therefore, Ferguson was able to spend these years throwing himself enthusiastically into a life of reading, writing and farming, on his old Perthshire estate at Bankhead and at his new home at Sciennes near Edinburgh—known, according to Henry Graham, 'from its remoteness and the chilly, fur-clad frame of its fiery occupant, by the name of "Kamtschatka"' (SML 108). Rapidly approaching his seventieth birthday, he issued another but rather fuller version of his Edinburgh lecture notes, entitled *Principles of Moral and Political Science* (1792), his last substantial publication. The following year, ever the intrepid adventurer, he set off on another lengthy journey through Europe—shrugging off his wife's nervousness on behalf of an elderly traveller and the inconvenient fact that Revolutionary France had just declared war on Britain. Passing through Flanders, Germany, Austria and Italy, he was able to collect in person some of the several distinctions he had been awarded by appreciative foreign societies—including the Berlin Academy of Sciences, the Etruscan Society of Antiquaries, the Florentine Academy and the Arcadia at Rome. As importantly, however, this journey gave Ferguson the chance to inspect at first hand many of the scenes to which his Roman history, now due to re-appear in a new edition, had made reference.

With his wife's death in March 1795 and having sold Bankhead, the philosopher also resolved to quit the Edinburgh scene entirely—where friends like Robertson and Smith were also now dead—and to settle himself at a new country estate at Hallyards in Peebles-shire. There he passed further long years of retirement, engaging in cattle-farming and haymaking, entertaining a succession of welcome houseguests (with Carlyle, Home and Sir John Macpherson among the most frequent), still reading prodigiously—including the poems of his young friend Walter Scott, George Vancouver's *Voyages* and John Robison's work on freemasonry—and communicating with authors and correspondents far and wide. It is also to this period that Cockburn's fond recollection of the retired academic, 'a singular apparition', wrapped against the cold, belongs: 'he looked like a philosopher from Lapland' (MOT 49). Finally, in the autumn of 1809, his hearing and eyesight both failing, Ferguson decided to remove for the last time, to St Andrews, then in the process of acquiring its modern reputation as a resort of genteel retirement. It was there that Adam Ferguson, the last surviving celebrity of the eighteenth-century Scottish Enlightenment, died peacefully on 22 February 1816, leaving his daughters, who surrounded the death-bed, to record a thought-provoking final utterance, hovering characteristically between the presbyterian certainties of his youth and the philosophical speculations of his later career: 'There *is* another world'.

Chapter Two

"The Basis of a Moral Nature":
The Teacher and the Moralist

During the course of this book, it will become clear that Adam Ferguson's most enduring achievement, by the end of an exceptionally long and fulfilling career as an active thinker and writer, was to have offered an essentially naturalistic account of man's existence in society. To this extent it should not be entirely surprising that by the mid-twentieth century, as we shall also see, he would have acquired a considerable reputation as an early prototype of the modern social scientist—by turns a pioneer of sociology and a visionary political theorist. But if one feature of Ferguson's intellectual career, as it gradually unfolded through the second half of the eighteenth century, should caution us against straightforward acceptance of these long-posthumous re-interpretations of his work, it is his unswerving devotion, as one of the Scottish Enlightenment's leading teachers of philosophy, to the traditional duties of moral instruction. For it bears endless repetition that Ferguson was, more than anything else, a moralist. Engaged in the crucial task of persuading people to re-think both their attitudes and their behaviour, he was preoccupied, first and foremost, with revealing to his readers and to successive generations of Edinburgh students the way in which the fundamentally *moral* qualities of men's actions should be understood. In other words, Ferguson, just like many of his closest Scottish friends and contemporaries who likewise combined a penchant for philosophical investigation with the obligations of university teaching, was in no sense the objective purveyor of a descriptive science of society. Rather he was—and we can be certain that he would have been blissfully content with the description—a shameless partisan for the cause of virtue. It is accordingly with his passionate concern with the moral dimension of man's life that any plausible account of Ferguson's activities as a whole must begin.

i

The importance of ethical issues to Ferguson's intellectual enterprise is best approached initially in the wider context of the endeavours in which so many of his intimate friends were also directly engaged. It is, after all, no concidence that, despite the rather different conclusions that they would reach about the moral grounds of our behaviour, Ferguson at Edinburgh and his friend Adam Smith at Glasgow, as well as eventually being hailed as two of the eighteenth century's most innovative social theorists, actually spent a significant part of their adult lives occupying chairs of moral philosophy in the Scottish universities. Nor is it an accident that other influential contributors to the "Science of Man", like Hutcheson in Glasgow, Thomas Reid in Aberdeen and later in Glasgow, and even Ferguson's own direct successor in Edinburgh, Dugald Stewart, served in this same demanding capacity. For the academic discipline of moral philosophy was, more than any other contemporary realm of inquiry, the rigorously-analytical foundation on which the Scottish Enlightenment as a whole would ultimately come to rest. It mattered a great deal, of course, in strictly practical terms, as indeed it did to Ferguson in particular—providing a prestigious title, a widely-respected instructional role and a reliable source of income. At the same time, however, moral philosophy served as the common intellectual fulcrum around which a diverse set of interests revolved. This was because, at least as it was understood in Scotland in Ferguson's day, moral philosophy entailed the search for convincing answers to some of the most important questions that could be asked about the human condition. Its existing assumptions, and particularly its familiar bones of contention, also supplied several of the widely-recognised starting-points from which it turned out, as the Scottish Enlightenment grew to maturity, that a variety of new investigations into other aspects of man's experiences might successfully be launched.

    In order fully to understand the central role that moral philosophy played in eighteenth-century Scotland, it is also necessary for us to recognise the considerable extent to which contemporaries still laboured in the long shadows cast by classical antiquity. The surviving works of Cicero, the most revered and most eloquent of all the ancient writers, had been among the most influential bodies of thought throughout Europe in the several centuries between the Renaissance and the Enlightenment: in particular, Cicero's compellingly rational and reasonable arguments on behalf of the obligation to live both actively and virtuously had resonated with enormous force among sixteenth- and seventeenth-century readers. Yet, for all the remarkable breadth of Cicero's own philosophical interests, ranging from a deep fascination with Academic scepticism to the detailed reconstruction of rhetorical theory, it is clear that he was most successful and most seminal in his attempts to popularise, especially through the treatises *De Officiis* and *De Finibus*, the distinctive moral vision of the Stoical thinkers of Greece and Rome. Indeed, as Ferguson himself would subsequently explain in the *Principles of Moral and Political Science*, in describing how the first of these two most widely-respected of ancient texts had originally come to be composed, when Cicero 'came to instruct his own son in the duties of morality, he seized on the principles of the Stoic philosophy, as the most applicable to the conduct of human life' (PI: 8).

To a great extent, however, the fruitful engagement that the academic philosophers of Ferguson's day were able to achieve with ancient Stoicism—an encounter that would in fact be rather closer than anything experienced by those who had taught the still-Aristotelian-oriented university curriculum of the seventeenth century—was also shaped by the somewhat ambiguous status of those ideas in broader European culture following the Renaissance. Not just the intensely-fashionable writings of Cicero but those of his successors Tacitus, Seneca, Epictetus and Marcus Aurelius Antoninus, some of them virtually unknown during the intervening fifteen hundred years, had inspired a motley assortment of sixteenth and early seventeenth-century imitators and copyists: these included but were by no means limited to the influential Flemish scholar Justus Lipsius, the French philosophers Guillaume du Vair and Marc-Antoine de Muret, the English statesman and historian Sir Walter Raleigh, his countryman the reflective bishop Joseph Hall, and, each of them active in their different ways in Jacobean and Caroline Scotland, the political writers George Buchanan, David Hume of Godscroft and Sir Robert Gordon of Gordonstoun. Yet neo-Stoicism, as it has come to be known, was certainly not unproblematical in its implications for moral philosophy. Indeed, this fact above all helps account for the very limited extent to which it had managed to penetrate the formal academic curriculum before the eighteenth century.

It was only too clear, for example, that certain Stoics—though, thankfully, not Cicero himself—had emphasised the unrelenting grip of Fate and destiny on men's affairs, thereby appearing to leave little scope for the exercise of free will that Christian moralists tended to prize. Some Stoics—notably Seneca and Epictetus—had even advocated the protection of one's own virtue by withdrawal from a dangerously corrupting world, seemingly implying in the process that active involvement in society was neither a necessary duty nor even particularly wise. Stoicism, in other words, for all its many attractions as a supremely elegant account of man's natural capacity for exhibiting moral behaviour in a social setting, turned out to be almost as capable of provoking a degree of understandable suspicion in modern audiences as it was of stimulating genuine admiration: in this regard, of course, its undeniably pagan origins had only proved a further incitement to hostile commentary, particularly after the Reformation. The result was that its precise usefulness in moral theory remained very much an unresolved issue among those thinkers of the Scottish Enlightenment—and, it would turn out, Ferguson not least—for whom the Stoics' approach to such questions exercised considerable fascination.

This long-running debate over the use and abuse of particular aspects of ancient thought, and especially the attempt from the early eighteenth century onwards to move Ciceronian ideas about moral education to the heart of the Scottish university syllabus, was, as we shall see, to have profound consequences for Ferguson's philosophy as it finally emerged to public view in Edinburgh in the 1760s. But it is at least as necessary that we appreciate the decisive intellectual impact of much more recent and more local disputes. For Francis Hutcheson's claims on behalf of the 'moral sense', the devastating riposte to them offered by David Hume, and then the various counter-attacks on Hume launched from within the Scottish professoriate, actually provide by far the most illuminating immediate context in which to explain Ferguson's priorities as a teacher of moral theory. Above all, in the wider history of philosophy, these Scottish arguments have to be seen as a collective response not so much to Stoicism's decidedly mixed bequest as to the far graver problems posed by the egotistical psychology of the English philosopher Thomas Hobbes, with its troubling assertions, embodied in the notorious *Leviathan* (1651), about the primacy of individual self-preservation in our decision-making and behaviour. Indeed, given the centrality of moral philosophy in Scotland's system of university education—it was, as we have noted, being rendered even more pivotal from the early decades of the eighteenth century—the need decisively to refute Hobbes's dangerously anti-social teachings and to provide a theologically-acceptable alternative account of human morality was obvious.

Hutcheson's efforts in this regard represented, as we saw in Chapter One, a veritable mainspring of the Scottish Enlightenment as a whole. Certainly his influence beyond the lecture halls of the University of

Glasgow was guaranteed not only by a series of noteworthy publications on philosophical topics but also by the dominant role in succeeding generations, both in the Church of Scotland and throughout Scottish academia, enjoyed by men, like the Moderate clergymen, who had been among his admiring pupils and most enthusiastic early readers. In Hutcheson's philosophy the reality of a 'moral sense' is a given. It is a necessary and unarguable feature of man's very nature. As we find him confidently asserting in the *Enquiry into the Original of our Ideas of Beauty and Virtue* (1725): 'the Moral Virtues have their Foundation in the Nature of Things' (EBV 196). But from this insistence all manner of other conclusions flow. Most importantly, an innate capacity for benevolence exists. Indeed, rather than being an instinctively inward-looking creature principally motivated by self-interest, man is in fact equipped with a powerful natural insight into the needs and interests of his fellows. Moreover, in responding to its promptings—in other words, in performing what are perceived as moral actions—it is possible, according to Hutcheson, both to earn and to enjoy the rightful approval of society, with all the rewards and pleasures that that entails. An even more far-reaching consequence of this naturalistic explanation of morality is, of course, that Hobbes's dark and dour psychology, recently re-stated by the English philosopher Bernard Mandeville in his *The Fable of the Bees* (1714), must also be fundamentally flawed: if morality is indeed rooted in our nature, it simply cannot be the case that, as Hutcheson disobligingly glosses Mandeville's subversive claims, 'the moral Virtues are the political Offspring, which Flattery begot upon Pride, i.e. that they are all a Chimera, an idle Fancy, a mere Trick' (EBV 1). For this reason, as the eighteenth century neared its middle years, it may have seemed to many of the younger generation of Scottish intellectuals, including Ferguson and his circle of talented Edinburgh friends, that Hutcheson, having built so prodigiously on the earlier achievements of several English thinkers, had in fact constructed the best-possible modern defence of religion and morality against all contrary claims.

Like most successful philosophical systems, however, the real difficulty with Hutcheson's neatly inter-locking arguments is that their overall persuasiveness rests ultimately upon a willingness to accept a number of key initial propositions: if these foundations of the structure are themselves undermined or even removed—if, for example, one simply denies that our propensity for making certain widely-approved moral judgments is in itself sufficient proof that they are an intrinsic feature of our nature—there is a serious risk that the whole edifice will begin to collapse under the impressive weight of its own logic. Such was the danger that was presented to Hutcheson's teachings, and so, in effect, to the core moral philosophy component in Scotland's academic curriculum, by Hume—a fact which, incidentally, also goes far to explain why it was that someone who is today recognised by many as the century's greatest original philosophical thinker was thwarted in his ambitions to become professor of moral philosophy at Edinburgh in 1745 and of logic at Glasgow in 1752. Indeed, Hume's scepticism seemed, if this were possible, almost more threatening to orthodox theories of morality than Hobbes's repellent egotism. For, whilst employing a philosophical approach that might initially have seemed perfectly acceptable to anyone accustomed to the methods that had delivered the reassuring conclusions of both John Locke in England and Hutcheson in Glasgow, Hume nevertheless manipulated it so aggressively that he was able to avoid arriving at many of their comforting assumptions about the operations of the mind. In consequence, he was also to place in serious doubt most of the detailed arguments about morality and human nature that had come to rest upon them.

Hume's contribution to the emerging mainstream tradition of eighteenth-century Scottish moral philosophy was therefore to test its foundations to breaking point—and, most later commentators have considered, very far beyond. In Hume's philosophy, as in that of his immediate British predecessors, the origins of our knowledge lie in experience alone: empirical in much the same way as Locke's or Hutcheson's, this approach insists that the human mind is formed as a *tabula rasa* (clean slate), onto which life and circumstances, their effects mediated through the senses which give us our only effective window on the world, inscribe all of the necessary information we eventually possess about our external environment. The really troubling aspect of Hume's acceptance of this perfectly respectable philosophical position, however, was that, unlike previous exponents, he was willing—eager, even—to push it to its logical conclusion. Indeed, it now became extremely difficult to avoid arriving at a position of outright scepticism. For since Greek antiquity there had been well-known and widely-credited criticisms of the operation of the senses and of their interaction with the conscious mind. Some thinkers, for example, had pointed out that the senses were often mistaken in the information that they provided. It was clear, too, that the human mind was capable of the wildest flights of imagination, some of which deluded people into believing the most improbable and unreasonable things. If, as Hume insisted, everything we think we know about our environment comes to us through this demonstrably imperfect route, then absolute certainty—even about the existence, let alone the detail, of the world around us—must always be illusory. As Hume puts it in the *Enquiry Concerning Human Understanding* (1748), in what is a characteristically provocative summary of where this extraordinary line of argument will eventually lead us, 'The falling of a pebble may, for ought we know, extinguish the Sun, or the wish of man control the planets in their orbits' (ECHU 164).

It was inevitable that such an extreme conclusion would be deeply troubling to those of Hume's contemporaries who were concerned with philosophical arguments about man and his place in the world. But an even more unsettling implication of Hume's vigorously sceptical brand of empiricism was the challenge that it posed to all conventional accounts of morality. Hutcheson, as we have just seen, was widely assumed to have exploded the egotists' arguments by recourse to something known as the 'moral sense', which seemed to root ethical judgments securely in human nature. Yet how could such a claim be reconciled with a wider philosophical system which asserts that the mind is in fact created as a *tabula rasa* and consequently teaches that all of our knowledge stems from experience alone? Unsurprisingly, given his ferocious logicality and willingness to entertain the most perplexing conclusions, Hume's answer is that this is simply not possible. In fact, he insists that it is necessary to consider moral reasoning not as an innate capacity implanted by nature but rather as a skill that we acquire—and, it is to be hoped, improve—through our education and experience. Indeed, as described by Hume, morality begins to appear little more than an elaborate social construct. Our conduct is itself the result of learning those particular behavioural traits which invariably win us the applause of observers: that which is moral is therefore, in Hume's arresting formulation in the *Enquiry Concerning the Principles of Morals* (1751), 'whatever mental action or quality gives to the spectator the pleasing sentiment of approbation' (ECHU 289).

For those accustomed to thinking of morality as a set of eternal absolutes prescribed by an inflexible God—let alone those who had recently been reassured by Hutcheson that its principles were indeed readily discernible to men by virtue of a reliable moral compass embedded in the very frame of their nature—Hume's account was utterly repugnant.

As perceptive contemporary critics were not slow to point out, Hume seemed at times very close to implying that behind every moral action actually lies nothing more than the self-interested pursuit of momentary popularity—even, perhaps, that morality itself amounts to whatever our current audience or immediate social circle say that it is. Smith's *Theory of Moral Sentiments* (1759), a work that directly influenced Ferguson's own moral teachings in the 1760s, was the next major Scottish contribution to the intensifying debate. It achieved fame with its ingenious claims that our morality, although not grounded in the 'moral sense' that his old teacher Hutcheson had identified, did actually rest upon a human facility for 'sympathy' which leads us to act in such a way as to win the approval of a hypothetical observer—the 'impartial spectator', as Smith dubbed him: 'Whatever may be the cause of sympathy', writes Smith, 'or however it may be excited, nothing pleases us more than to observe in other men a fellow-feeling with all the emotions of our own breast' (TMS 10). Hume's alarming assertions also gave rise to a number of less experimental responses. To James Balfour, Ferguson's immediate professorial predecessor at Edinburgh, the obvious solution was simply the shrill re-statement of convention: 'it is certain at least', blustered Balfour in 1763, 'that the difference betwixt virtue and vice is strongly founded in nature' (DM 4). Others, however, understood the need to go much further than this, and to seek a route which either demolished or at least by-passed the immense obstacle to the traditional understanding of morality that Hume's disturbingly cogent work undeniably represented.

In many ways the two impressive Aberdonian thinkers Thomas Reid and George Campbell, together with their rather less decorous but more lionised colleague James Beattie, chose the latter course, providing in the process what many were ready to welcome at the time as a necessary restorative for the battered and bruised state in which Hume's brutal assaults appeared to have left moral theory. Reid in particular was a worthy opponent for Hume—whom Reid, in a move which speaks volumes for the affable relations possible within the peculiarly incestuous social world of the Scottish philosophers, even asked to check the page-proofs of some of his work before its final publication. Reid's intellectual strategy was also adventurous. For, rather than simply tackling Hume on his own ground, and engaging in yet another careful re-working of conventional empiricist claims about the uncertain basis of our sensory perception, Reid moved the philosophical argument in an entirely new direction. In effect, he abandoned the psychological models, whose vulnerability to sceptical exploitation had been revealed so alarmingly by Hume, that had been taken for granted by earlier authorities like Locke and Hutcheson. In their place, particularly in his *Inquiry into the Human Mind on the Principles of Common Sense* (1764), Reid sought to defend the accuracy and the trustworthiness of the senses. In arguments which defer continually to our everyday experiences and commonplace perceptions, he insists that, when we believe something to be sound and reasonable, it invariably is so. The continual stream of impressions and sensations that crowd in upon our consciousness, which for Hume supply merely the illusion of true knowledge, do actually constitute a real and reliable basis for our understanding of the world. As Ferguson himself described Reid's contribution, looking back with the clarity available to an observer of the debate by the 1790s, he 'taught us to state the facts, of which we are conscious, not in figurative language, but in the terms which are proper to the subject': as a result, 'The reality of knowledge... however little to be explained by any corporeal analogy, may be safely assumed, and the facts which relate to the attainment of it, be considered as an important part in the history of mind' (PI: 75–6).

The argument sketched out by Reid, as beautiful as it was simple, was particularly seductive because it seemed to provide an account of the operations of the human mind which, unlike Hume's, was fully in tune with our intuitive assumptions about the secure grip that we possess upon external reality. For these reasons, as well as because of its deliberate conformity with traditional Christian ideas about our in-built capacity for moral judgment, it was also able to dominate philosophical instruction, and consequently the university curriculum, not only in Scotland but also in parts of Europe and in North America, deep into the nineteenth century. Reinforced by the extraordinary public reputation that Beattie achieved with his disingenuously-titled *Essay on Truth* (1770), which was really just a blistering attack upon Hume's work, as well as by Campbell's more measured critique of religious scepticism, "Common Sense" philosophy, as it rapidly became known, was an identifiably Scottish invention which effectively demarcated a protected space within which a conventional moral theory could still be safely elaborated. In such a system, and according to arguments that would in some respects have been as recognisable to Cicero and Seneca as to Hutcheson himself (who, as Ferguson was careful to emphasise, had also 'revered' the Stoics), morality comprised either the willing performance

or the conscious neglect of certain duties (P I:8). Virtue consisted in the
honest attempt to live life in accordance with clear and unvarying rules.
And moral judgment was identified with the exercise of an instinctive
mental faculty by which those rules could be reliably discerned and followed: in the intentionally soothing words of George Turnbull, another
Aberdonian scholar who saw things from very much the standpoint of
Hutcheson, it was necessary, as well as perfectly possible, for men to continue to believe that 'We have... by nature a moral sense' (TAP 132).

ii

When Ferguson asks where our perceptions of morality really come from,
it will now be clear that this, in Scotland in the 1760s, in the aftermath
of Hume's shocking arguments, was necessarily the most heavily-loaded
of questions. Indeed, it is difficult to avoid the thought that this fundamental aspect of Ferguson's thought was simply the carefully-calibrated
response of a Scottish academic philosopher and university teacher to
the raging controversies among his compatriots over the origin and
nature of morality. Certainly, with experience of the militia dispute and
of the *Douglas* and Ossian affairs already under his belt, Ferguson was
by this time a practised—and, at least outwardly, a supremely confident—polemicist: in the black arts of advancing a contentious case and
subjecting a range of opposing arguments to withering criticism, none
of Scotland's moral theorists was quite so seasoned when he finally made
his first intervention in the philosophical debate. Moreover, Ferguson
had clearly realised by the time that the *Essay* appeared—as Smith had
probably realised rather earlier—that the task of sketching a full-blown
history of man's development in society was actually a necessary part of
the wider enterprise of moral philosophy as that subject had increasingly
come to be understood. For it was evident that, without detailed reference to the various social and cultural environments in which human
beings find themselves, it would be impossible to resolve the kinds of
problems about the foundations of morality and behaviour that recent
theorists had begun to identify. It is this seminal realisation—in effect,
marking a key junction point at which the conventional agenda for
academic moral philosophy really begins to broaden out into an inter-
disciplinary "Science of Man"—which explains ultimately why the
Essay, whose historical and quasi-sociological elements have tended to

monopolise the attention of most recent commentators, also contains so much discussion of issues recognisably related to the contemporary Scottish debates over moral theory.

Above all, it is to this intensely-polemical context that we must attribute the way in which, in the crucial sixth section of Part I of the *Essay*, titled simply 'Of Moral Sentiment', Ferguson chooses to present the absolutely key supposition, unmistakably Hutchesonian in inspiration, that a capacity for moral judgment is an integral and distinctive feature of human nature. Indeed, characteristically emphasising rather than obscuring the bitter acrimony which had lately come to surround this claim, Ferguson obliges his readers to reflect for a moment upon the contrary proposition—by implication the grim vision of Hobbes and his disciples—that men, other than their manifestly greater facility for tool-making and invention, are not really all that different from the animals:

Is man therefore, in respect to his object, to be classed with the mere brutes, and only to be distinguished by faculties that qualify him to multiply contrivances for the support and convenience of animal life, and by the extent of a fancy that renders the care of animal preservation to him more burdensome than it is to the herd with which he shares in the bounty of nature? (E 35)

We are rapidly disabused of such notions, however. For Ferguson hints strongly at the evidence—which, significantly, he insists is to be found not in abstract reasoning but in the concrete history of man in society—for our ability to think beyond these narrow confines of material gain and self-interest:

If this were his case, the joy which attends on success, or the griefs which arise from disappointment, would make the sum of his passions. The torrent that wasted, or the inundation that enriched his possessions, would give him all the emotion with which he is seized, on the occasion of a wrong by which his fortunes are impaired, or of a benefit by which they are preserved and enlarged. His fellow-creatures would be considered merely as they affected his interest. Profit or loss would serve to mark the event of every transaction; and the epithets *useful* or *detrimental* would serve to distinguish his mates in society, as they do the tree which bears plenty of fruit, from that which serves only to cumber the ground, or intercept his view. (E 35–6)

In other words, the way in which man is actually seen to behave in his dealings with other members of the species suggests that he is endowed by nature with far more penetrating insights and sensibilities than the stark and one-dimensional Hobbesian view of things would appear to allow.

From this typically pugnacious starting-point, with Ferguson seeming almost to relish the opportunity to brandish the rival theory before ruthlessly dismembering it in front of our eyes, he proceeds to construct in its place his own much less perplexing interpretation of the natural origins of morality. It is plain, says Ferguson, again seeking to link his moral argument with the evidence of man's history as a social being, that Hobbes's version of how man's psychology was first formed simply does not square with what the common experience of mankind through the ages has revealed: as the *Essay* puts this point in terms which once more hint at the intimate relationship in Ferguson's mind between moral philosophy and the study of society's evolution over time, it is simply 'not the history of our species'. Instead, the accumulated evidence of man's experience in all its varied forms supports the view that he does indeed possess an innate capacity for moral judgment of the sort that Hutcheson and Reid had both described—something which, in the pithy phrase of Ferguson's older friend in Edinburgh, the influential legal philosopher and historian Lord Kames, might be thought of as 'a common sense of mankind with respect to right and wrong' (SHM II:252).

As Ferguson also seeks to emphasise in the *Essay*, in a notably fluent and convincing piece of prose oratory which smacks of the Edinburgh lecture-theatre in which he must often have declaimed to his students on this very question, man is equipped with an acute sensitivity to the feelings, actions and interests of his fellow humans. In fact, this is actually so powerful and so instinctive that it can operate even when those people are far distant from our own place and time—even, oddly, when they are merely figments of the creative imagination:

As actors or spectators, we are perpetually made to feel the difference of human conduct, and from a bare recital of transactions which have passed in ages and countries remote from our own, are moved with admiration and pity, or transported with indignation and rage. Our sensibility on this subject gives their charm, in retirement, to the relations of history, and to the fictions of poetry; sends forth the tear of compassion, gives to the blood its briskest movement, and to the eye its liveliest glances of displeasure or joy. It turns human life into an interesting spectacle, and perpetually solicits even the indolent to mix, as opponent or friends, in the scenes which are acted before them. Joined to the powers of deliberation and reason, it constitutes the basis of a moral nature; and whilst it dictates the terms of praise and of blame, serves to class our fellow-creatures by the most admirable and engaging, or the most odious and contemptible, denominations. (E 36)

The operation of this 'sensibility', then, not only coaxes us continually into social encounters—a key deduction which, incidentally, meshes perfectly with Ferguson's related claims, which we shall need to consider much more closely in the next chapter, about the irresistible human yearning for society. At the same time, it is linked directly with our evidently innate capacity for calculation and judgment—which is to say, with our natural power of reason—which must therefore be understood as having an essentially moral dimension of its own. Indeed, as Ferguson finally sums up this fundamental premise on which his moral theory rests, in a memorable phrase which the previous decades' philosophical debates in Scotland must have rendered pregnant with meaning for most of the *Essay*'s early readers, this extraordinary human facility for distinguishing right from wrong is an in-built characteristic of the human species: it represents, quite simply, 'the basis of a moral nature'.

iii

Whilst firmly grounding his system of morality in the frame of human nature, Ferguson's other initial concern, again clearly a response to the prior discussions of Hutcheson, Hume, Smith and Reid, was to try to establish the precise connection between our own moral perceptions and the evident expectations and judgments of our fellow members of society. To put this slightly differently, Ferguson was fascinated, like the other Scottish theorists of his time, and indeed like all earlier thinkers in touch with the Stoic tradition, by the ways in which man's membership of a community impacts not only upon his conduct but even upon his very consciousness of moral considerations themselves. Importantly, this aspect of Ferguson's thought, which can be regarded as part of the necessary philosophical preparation before the elaboration of a coherent system of moral instruction, also reveals something of the continuing influence of Joseph Addison's writings, with their characteristic probing and promotion of what eighteenth-century people usually described simply as 'politeness'—which was to say, that refined, reasonable and essentially tolerant social disposition widely believed to characterise the fortunate inhabitants of complex and advanced polities such as modern Britain. As we have seen, Ferguson, like all of the Moderate clergymen, had been from his youth an ardent admirer of Addison, and particularly of *The Spectator*, a seminal publication in which many of the timeless problems of inter-personal relations, including the fraught business of being expected by society to exhibit appropriate behaviour, had been examined in a beguiling modern philosophical idiom that was simultaneously consoling and thought-provoking. It should therefore really be no surprise that 'Mr Addison' is actually the first author to whom Ferguson explicitly returns in the preliminary section of his mature philosophical work, the *Principles*; nor, indeed, that Ferguson's account of the foundations of morality, as variously expressed in the *Essay* and the *Institutes*, strives continually to establish the relationship between our own sensitivity to ethical considerations and the prospects of our being likely to win social approval (P I:3).

In setting out to explore how the morally-correct and the socially-acceptable might be connected, however, it is clear that Ferguson, as well as deferring to the polite literature of Augustan England, was also revealing his indebtedness to some extremely well-known philosophical inquiries in antiquity. Indeed, it had long been argued, and, once again, particularly by the Stoics, that we should pursue virtue not because of the rewards that it might eventually secure for us in this (or in the next) life, nor even because of the punishments that failure to be virtuous might attract. Rather we should behave virtuously in society simply because we have an absolute obligation, as humans, to seek to act in a way which is morally correct. In this view, which Cicero had powerfully endorsed in *De Officiis*, to act morally is to do nothing more than to perform our duty: in an important sense, that which is virtuous is merely that which is appropriate and necessary to our condition as humans. As a result, Ferguson was in fact seeking to achieve yet another entirely familiar philosophical goal, with many outstanding precedents among previous theorists, when in the *Institutes*, that terse but revealing digest of his Edinburgh moral philosophy course, he deftly linked the ethical with the socially-sanctioned by means of the concept of 'probity'. For this, as Ferguson explains, 'is the most approved disposition; and the external expressions of probity, the most approved actions. These constitute the whole, or the most essential part, of virtue.' (I 111)

It will be clear, however, that it was also necessary for Ferguson at least to define 'probity' rather more precisely if this critical hinge-point in his own account of virtue, seeming to achieve a fruitful connection between our performance of truly moral actions and the fulfilment of our social obligations, were to make possible a coherent foundation for a system of practical instruction. And in fact, just a few pages earlier in the *Institutes*, he had already prepared the ground for this strategy by explaining that

> Men who regard the rights, and feel for the sufferings, of others; who are ever ready to do acts of kindness; who are faithful and true to the expectations they raise,—are said to have probity. (I 106)

Ferguson, in other words, insisted that the main characteristic of probity, itself understood as the chief expression of virtue, is nothing other than a sincere and sympathetic concern for the needs and interests of our fellows. It follows from this, of course, that what we think of as moral conduct is necessarily concerned with the performance of those essentially benevolent duties which earn us the sincere approval of society. Moreover, if this train of reasoning would have seemed to his better-informed Edinburgh students like just one more way of arriving at Hutcheson's well-established claims on behalf of the 'moral sense', and ultimately only an alternative route back to Shaftesbury, then Ferguson was not remotely interested in concealing its orientation. On the contrary, in another striking passage in the *Institutes* that can only have been meant to signal very clearly to his students the securely orthodox position that this argument would allow them to stake out within an otherwise violently-contested field, Ferguson observes that 'we may venture to affirm, that benevolence, or the law of society, combined with the law of estimation, is the principle of moral approbation; and that to bestow our esteem on virtue, is to love mankind'—this summarising sentence being explicitly footnoted to the familiar writings of Shaftesbury. (I 114–5)

At the same time, on the evidence left to us in the *Institutes*, Ferguson seems to have concluded the several consecutive sections of the Edinburgh moral philosophy course that deal specifically with the connections between moral judgments and their social context with what sound remarkably like some of the claims for man's natural gregariousness and sociability that he would himself reiterate elsewhere in print— most notably in the opening sections of the *Essay* (and which we shall again need to explore in greater detail in the next chapter): 'Man', the professor insisted to his students, 'is by nature a member of society...' (I 115). Indeed, it is this other seminal result of man's basic instincts which means that self-preservation on the one hand, and 'the law of society' on the other, are, despite the strenuous denials of certain other theorists, fully reconcileable. As Ferguson explains what is a crucial deduction in terms of the existing debate:

> his safety, and his enjoyment, require that he should be preserved what he is by nature; his perfection consists in the excellency or measure of his natural abilities and dispositions, or, in other words, it consists in his being an excellent part of the system to which he belongs. (I 115)

It is intolerable, says Ferguson, for us to suppose that our manifest desire for self-preservation in any way detracts from our ability to act ordinarily with probity and benevolence. Nor is it plausible, as philosophers like Hobbes argue, that there is a preponderant disposition towards self-preservation which gives rise naturally to a whole range of fundamentally anti-social traits. For as a creature formed for society, our individual interests must necessarily be capable of reconciliation with those of our fellows: in Ferguson's definitive words on a question which had been the focal point of so much controversy, 'the effect should be the same, whether the individual means to preserve himself, or to preserve his community: with either intention he must cherish the love of mankind, as the most valuable part of his character' (I 116). And it is also this, Ferguson concludes, which elevates the performance of social duty to the status of a genuinely virtuous action: in short, it 'leads men to give to probity, as such, the preference to every other disposition or habit of mind'.

iv

With a general principle of probity or benevolence as the very cornerstone of moral philosophy and, at the same time, as an essential psychological focus of man's motivation and decision-making, Ferguson was able to unfold a system of practical morality that was at once much wider in application and much more specific in its focus. Indeed, this task seems to have occupied a substantial proportion of the lecture course that Ferguson was delivering at Edinburgh by the later 1760s. In fact, these concerns eventually filled the fourth of the seven parts of the syllabus, eventually forming in the *Institutes* the second-longest element in the printed text (running to more than fifty closely-argued pages) and, lest anyone misunderstand the importance of linking principle with practice, placed under the self-explanatory heading 'Of Moral Laws, and their most general Applications' (I 138). Here, however, the refutation of Hobbes and Hume and the veneration of Hutcheson, the unmistakably polemical intentions behind the broad shape and structure of his moral philosophy, are finally left behind. Instead, Ferguson's main concern as a practical moralist is with advancing the specific moral doctrines of Stoicism, which, as we have seen, had long been recognised as providing a useful account of the way in which particular judgments about our conduct in society are actually derived.

Ferguson's debts to the Stoics are to some extent confirmed even out of his own mouth. For, in a very rare autobiographical allusion in the early pages of the *Principles*, he offers his readers the gently self-deprecating revelation that 'The Author, in some of the statements which follow, may be thought partial to the Stoic philosophy', though he is also careful to add, just in case anyone mistake this for a rash admission of inflexibility, that he was 'not conscious of having warpt the truth to suit any system whatever' (PI: 7). At the same time, Ferguson's indebtedness to Stoicism can be seen very plainly in his intertextual references. Indeed, it is clear that, especially in the heavily-footnoted pages of the *Institutes*, ancient authorities such as Cicero, Marcus Aurelius and, above all, Epictetus, greatly outnumber the modern philosophers. But Ferguson's reliance upon the Stoics is perhaps most evident in the general form taken by the developing argument about the proper analysis of human behaviour, as well as in several of the specific points made. In fact, he elects to begin the substantive discussion of practical morality in the *Institutes* with a section entitled simply 'Of Good and Evil in general', in which Cicero's *De Finibus* is the guiding influence. Significantly, it is also the Stoics' authoritative analysis of this whole area of perennial moral debate over which Ferguson lingers longest and most fondly. As he explains:

The Stoics maintained, that nothing was to be classed under the predicament of good, but what was at all times invariably to be chosen.

That nothing was to be classed under the predicament of evil, but what was at all times invariably to be shunned, or rejected.

That to call that good which ought at any time to be rejected, or that evil which ought at any time to be chosen, was not only absurd in terms, but tended to weaken the resolution with which a man ought always to make his choice. (I 143–4)

On this evidence, it is clear that the Stoics' characteristically sharp distinction between good and evil—permitting no ambiguity and tolerating no special-pleading or casuistry at the margins—represents the secure and familiar baseline for Ferguson's own prescriptions.

Yet Ferguson was also concerned, like both the Stoics and most of their later admirers, with those natural consequences of our actions which, in conformity with the general principles of morality, we find ourselves wishing either to attain or to avoid. As Ferguson enumerates them straightforwardly in the *Institutes*, they amount simply to 'Life and Death, Pleasure and Pain, Excellence and Defect, Happiness and Misery': it follows, of course, that we have very different attitudes towards each half of these pairs of opposing experiences, themselves the inevitable result of the operation of what he calls 'the physical laws of self-preservation, of society, or of estimation' (I 145). Ferguson was not, however, equally concerned with each of these sets of alternative outcomes. Rather, and again because of their significance within the continuing Scottish controversy over the 'moral sense', he devoted the greatest attention to a discussion of 'Pleasure and Pain' as rival motivating concerns. As Ferguson reports, after a lengthy circuit around the miscellaneous forms of sensual and intellectual gratification that appear to await us, the greatest enjoyment is ultimately derived from virtuous behaviour: 'It appears', he concludes, 'on the whole, that just opinions, benevolent affections, and serious engagements, are the preferable enjoyments of human nature' (I 155).

Ferguson reinforces this point by emphasising the importance of 'Excellence and Defect' in our moral calculations. As he insists, purposely listing in the process several of the key virtues classically treated in Cicero's *De Officiis*, 'The excellence of a man is probity, supported by wisdom, temperance, and fortitude. Probity is the love of mankind' (I 155). In other words, the perfection that we are impelled to seek consists in the exercise of benevolence, itself the highest expression of virtue. Nor should the moral implications of our natural interest in 'Happiness and Misery' be underestimated: defined by Ferguson as 'the state of greatest enjoyment of which human nature is susceptible', it too is simply the natural result of our acting in a manner that is 'benevolent, wise, and courageous' (I 157–8). As Ferguson concludes, at the same time reaffirming once more the explicitly Stoical assumptions upon which this system of morality is founded: 'This is what Epictetus and Antoninus meant, by saying, "That virtue is the sole good". Unhappy is he who understands their meaning, and yet can treat it with scorn' (I 159). In short, true happiness, which by our nature we are compelled to seek, is merely the inevitable consequence for the individual of favouring those modes of behaviour that the Stoics have shown to be both moral and proper for a human being.

With appropriate conduct therefore delivering not only a sense of enjoyment but some hopes of moving towards both excellence and happiness in the longer term, Ferguson also finds it necessary to explore in further detail what he calls the 'degrees of Happiness, and the means of Improvement' (I 162). Even here, however, Stoicism is not very far from his thoughts (and nor, as we shall see in Chapter 5, is man's propensity for engagement in politics, a specific form of behaviour through which Ferguson considers that we can actually approach the genuine satisfaction and fulfilment that we naturally crave). The characteristic stress of the Stoics upon man's deficiencies runs strongly through Ferguson's handling of this topic: as he puts it, 'Men conceive perfection, but are capable only of improvement' (I 162). Often, indeed, our lot is to be truly miserable, a situation which, again with telling references to Epictetus and Marcus Aurelius, Ferguson hammers home in the *Institutes* with great rhetorical force (I 165). But conversely, progress towards happiness is itself possible if we 'rely only on what is in our own power'—which is to say, as Ferguson explains it, if we 'have continually in view, that we are members of society, and of the community of mankind' (I 169). As Ferguson re-states this same argument in terms of a quotation which nicely captures some of the attractions of Stoic ideas for Christian thinkers, '*I am in the station which God has assigned me*, says Epictetus'. Once having attained this condition, the demonstrable connection between the good and the proper will ensure that, in following our duty and performing our allotted roles, we shall inevitably find ourselves behaving virtuously. Finally underlining this argument, Ferguson reminds us of a related point that he has already established at length elsewhere: 'The greatest good competent to man's nature, is the love of mankind' (I 171). In other words, on what is still recognisably Stoical reasoning, such happiness as is available to us in an imperfect world can best be pursued by acting altruistically, in accordance with the benevolent disposition of our moral nature.

Yet for all his undoubted admiration for their treatment of man's natural moral faculties and sociable inclinations, Ferguson's attitude towards the Stoics, like that of most of their other modern devotees, was by no means uncritical. Much of the difficulty inevitably turned out to consist in the quietism intrinsic to the teachings of some of the leading Roman Stoics—even though in many ways this was, of course, merely a logical deduction from their entirely uncontroversial insistence upon man's imperfection. In essence, this had often led Stoics to imply that passivity might itself be preferable to activity, a claim that was necessarily hard to square with a recognisably Christian approach to practical morality in which a man's prime duty to strive for virtue is usually taken for granted. More troubling still from Ferguson's point of view, it was all but impossible for an eighteenth-century philosopher to reconcile the conventional Stoical stress upon patient endurance of one's allotted situation in life with an emerging Enlightenment characterisation of the species in which men's unceasing activity, ingenuity and ambition for change was coming to be identified, as we shall see in the next chapter, as the key causal influence in the progressive civilisation and enrichment of the species. In this matter, indeed, there is no doubt that Ferguson's own sympathies lay firmly on the side of the moderns. He believed that mankind's natural inclination, especially at those crucial moments where history was literally in the making, had been to be dynamic, forceful and acquisitive rather than static, meek and acquiescent: 'Man is by nature an artist, endowed with ingenuity, discernment, and will', as he affirms, without any discernible hint of doubt or regret, in the *Principles* (P I:200).

Perhaps inevitably, this departure from one central aspect of the Stoic legacy is somewhat less overt in the *Institutes*, a work of academic moral philosophy which owes a great deal to the ethical framework of Stoicism, than in the *Essay* in particular, which is concerned much more with explaining how man had successfully advanced from primitiveness to civilisation. In the *Institutes*, Ferguson does in fact offer a number of remarks which clearly assume that individuals are by nature active and progressive: for example, in the opening part of the syllabus, under the suggestive heading 'The natural history of Man', Ferguson emphasises the characteristic propensity of the human species, unlike other animals, to seek to occupy a variety of environments and then successfully to adapt themselves to each (I 16–17). It is principally in the *Essay*, however, where the analysis of man's development in society is the governing preoccupation, that Ferguson again and again expresses a profoundly un-Stoical belief in the unique blessings which man's natural impatience and ambition have conferred upon the species as a whole. Indeed, in undoubtedly one of the most gloriously sweeping passages that he ever composed, Ferguson treats his readers to a majestic vision of man as compulsive self-improver, the whole tenor of the pictures he conjures up constituting a tacit but unanswerable refutation of the faith of many ancient Stoics in the superiority of personal contentment and inward equanimity:

> He is in some measure the artificer of his own frame, as well as his fortune, and is destined, from the earliest age of his being, to invent and contrive. He applies the same talents to a variety of purposes, and acts nearly the same part in very different scenes. He would always be improving on his subject, and he carries this intention where-ever he moves, through the streets of the populous city, or the wilds of the forest. While he appears equally fitted to every condition, he is upon this account unable to settle in any. At once obstinate and fickle, he complains of innovations, and is never sated with novelty. He is perpetually busied in reformation, and is continually wedded to his errors. If he dwell in a cave, he would improve it into a cottage; if he has already built, he would still build to a greater extent. (E 12)

Such enticing images of unrelenting human drive and inventiveness—qualities for which Ferguson's admiration and enthusiasm are here so unbounded as to be almost audible—can also have left his contemporaries, themselves attuned to the progressive values and expansive vision of the Enlightenment, in little doubt. An ambition for advancement and a capacity for continual adaptation are not only natural in mankind. They are also wholly desirable. Stoicism has—literally—a great many virtues to recommend it as the basis of practical morality, particularly in providing compelling arguments in favour of the regulation and essential moderation of inter-personal behaviour. But where Ferguson's moral philosophy ultimately gives way to the preoccupations of the historian and the social theorist, the Stoical values of patience and forbearance are necessarily abandoned for the even more necessary virtues of well-directed creativity and ambition.

v

As we have seen, the practice of moral philosophy was not only a professional obligation for Adam Ferguson during his career as a university teacher. In the final analysis, it was the intellectual foundation for all of his far-reaching inquiries about man and society. It prompted many of the questions about the nature of mankind that he would want to ask. It motivated many of the specific controversies in which he would wish to become embroiled. It drew him instinctively to certain preceding traditions of argument and analysis whilst leading him emphatically to reject others. It even united him, sometimes in a strange sort of friendly rivalry, with a handful of his closest lifelong associates. Indeed, the sheer ubiquity and importance of moral philosophy in eighteenth-century Scotland's intellectual life, as well as in the contemporary re-development of the Scottish universities, means that we can scarcely consider ourselves properly finished with it at this early stage. For many aspects of Ferguson's historical work and political outlook were, as we shall continue to find, closely bound up with its pervasive influence; and, not least because of the ambivalent relationship with ancient Stoicism into which it also turned out to have delivered him, we shall see again and again that it helped to shape other distinctive aspects of his thought. As a teacher and writer, then, Ferguson was more than anything else formed by his obligations—and, it has to be said, by his acute anxieties—as a moral philosopher. But it is to his ultimately more famous interests in social theory, and to his seminal conclusions as a student of man in society, that we now turn.

Chapter Three

"From Rudeness to Civilization": The Theorist of Society

If one aspect of Adam Ferguson's thought above all others reveals the extent but also the limits of his originality as a theorist, it must be his preoccupation with the evolution and nature of human society—an investigation which, as we have already seen, grew out of but also transcended and transformed his professional interests as a university teacher and moral philosopher. Certainly the questions that Ferguson was now led to ask belong as much to what would eventually be recognised as the realm of advanced social theory as they do to the conventional idioms of moral philosophy as these had evolved by the mid-eighteenth century. For example, how had the extraordinarily complex network of interpersonal relationships within which we live first emerged? What do the essential characteristics of human society reveal about our distinctive biological and psychological traits as a species? How might the remarkable variations in customs and institutions that arise between different human societies be explained? How far do geography and the environment influence the evolution of society in all its many forms? Is the progressive development of mankind in material and technological terms paralleled by equivalent advances in moral refinement and political organisation? Most intriguingly of all, perhaps, might some important aspects of our progress even turn out to be reversible in certain conditions, or at least carry with them important drawbacks and disadvantages? A burning desire to construct plausible answers to these and related inquiries turned out to be central to the activities of Adam Ferguson both as a teacher and as a thinker. It is no accident that they became central also to the intellectual agenda of the Scottish—and so of the European—Enlightenment as a whole.

i

Ferguson's interest in the origins and nature of human society was not only a natural outgrowth from his concerns as a moral philosopher. In an important sense its roots also lay deep in the intellectual history of western Europe—a history with which Ferguson, who, as we have seen, was at least as well-read as any of his voraciously bookish contemporaries, was thoroughly familiar. Whether found, for instance, in the timeless writings of Aristotle, with their definitive analysis of the various forms of government and communal organisation known to antiquity, or in the works of Cicero, which perfectly exemplified the Stoics' interest in the fragmentary evidence for mankind's earliest social arrangements, all moral philosophers of Ferguson's era acknowledged an ancestry for their own speculations about human society that was as luminous as it was ancient. It was clear, moreover, that the first stages of society had always been of interest to successive generations of theorists precisely because of the light that they promised to shed upon how political structures in particular had evolved. Certainly it had never been in doubt among European writers that, if a specific custom or institution could be shown to have enjoyed prolonged usage, its authority would be much enhanced: indeed, if it could be traced back to the situation in which the earliest humans had existed, then its legitimacy might well become effectively unassailable. Such modes of thought, in which precedent appeared the ultimate winning argument, go far towards explaining the obsessive concern among theorists, intensifying even further from the Renaissance onwards, for tracing the circumstances in which the constitutional and judicial structures still evident in modern societies had originally been arrived at.

For this reason it is in the first instance to the great political and legal commentators of the sixteenth and seventeenth centuries, and to the essentially historical inquiries in which they had become engaged, that we should look if we wish to understand the intellectual background to Ferguson's own fascination with the evolution of human society. And this is true in relation not only to the substantive questions that were increasingly being asked but also to the distinctive methods and techniques that were beginning to be utilised. Above all, an interest in accumulating vast quantities of documentary evidence about earlier societies had characterised much post-Renaissance scholarship of this kind. Jean Bodin's *Six Books of the Republic* (1576), for example, was in its own time a contribution to the quest for order during the French civil wars that subsequently came to be seen chiefly as a notorious apology for the emerging phenomenon of absolute monarchy. Yet Bodin himself is reputed to have spent no less than ten years poring over the historical records before finally feeling able to publish this most seminal of political texts. The result was a study which rested on a wealth of examples culled equally from the Bible, from classical antiquity, and from the medieval and modern histories of the European and non-European worlds. The way that his theories about the origins and evolution of different constitutional arrangements were so clearly underpinned by an immense body of historical proofs—presented to its readers as nothing less than a pure distillation of the totality of human experience—also rendered Bodin's achievement exceptionally influential among later writers. Indeed, so much of a pointer to the future would the *Six Books* later come to seem that Dugald Stewart, Ferguson's star pupil and a distinguished Edinburgh professor in his own right when he succeeded his mentor in 1785, was undoubtedly right to discern in Bodin's extraordinary effort 'a strong resemblance to that afterwards pursued by Montesquieu' (DEGV I:40).

A rather different ideological motivation but very similar methodological framework was exhibited in the early seventeenth century in the work of Hugo Grotius, the great Dutch philosopher and legal theorist. Grotius's masterpiece, *On the Rights of War and Peace* (1625), remains a landmark in the history of European jurisprudence, asserting as it does, with unrivalled clarity and force, the timeless existence of laws of nature. Indeed, Grotius went somewhat further than this, suggesting that these God-given precepts had also shaped the institutions and values of all people in all ages: their fundamental influence could therefore be traced, as Grotius attempted to show, through a careful study of a vast range of historical evidence. His intentions in this scholarly enterprise were in fact both immediate and intensely polemical. In particular, he wished to promote adherence, in an era of widespread Continental warfare, to those widely-approved restraints upon the actions of individual lawmakers and sovereign states that have subsequently come to be known as international law: the laws of nature, on this reasoning, embody the lowest common denominator of right and wrong by which all rational humans should be able to agree to be bound. Yet Grotius, like Bodin before him, would exercise even more authority over succeeding generations of intellectuals as a social theorist than as a lawyer. For he had in effect shown once again how an historically-grounded analysis of human society, encompassing the full range of past experiences, could yield a hugely-persuasive account of the origins and nature of man's most significant institutions.

France and the Netherlands had thus provided some of the most imaginative and influential contributions to the study of society to emerge prior to the eighteenth century. But England too, especially after around 1650, produced work of the first importance that would directly shape the Enlightenment's subsequent philosophical development. Almost inevitably given its fiendish complexity, the interpretation of Hobbes's *Leviathan*, as we have already seen, remains contentious. It is certain, however, that it reinforced contemporaries' growing fascination with the problem of the origins and nature of human communities. For Hobbes had advanced a highly idiosyncratic account of what the earliest ages of history—here dubbed 'the state of nature'—were actually like. Indeed, whereas Cicero, for example, had sketched a comparatively bland picture of the supposedly isolated existence of individual men before the original formation of society, Hobbes, writing in the uncertain aftermath of the English civil wars and revolution of the 1640s, in which traditional power-structures had been subverted and 'the world turned upside-down', came to the alternative and extraordinarily bleak conclusion that the earliest times, before the initial imposition of any meaningful social and political authority, must in fact have been marked by unrestrained and unceasing conflict among men.

Brutal competition between self-regarding individuals, at least according to Hobbes, was therefore the natural order of things in human affairs. It was merely the inevitable consequence, in a situation without the smack of firm government, of the equal capacities and no less equal jealousies and desires with which nature had apparently endowed all of mankind. And it was precisely to escape these horrifying natural circumstances, Hobbes insisted, that men had subsequently entered into a contract with one another to submit themselves collectively to the protective authority of an absolute and unchallengeable sovereign, himself emphatically not party to that agreement but rather its awe-inspiring and strictly non-negotiable enforcer: 'society, altogether unnatural to its members', as Ferguson unsympathetically glossed the conclusion that Hobbes had finally reached, 'is to be established and preserved by force' (P I:197). Needless to say, very little about Hobbes's profoundly disturbing account of man's brutish individualism, and of the role of social institutions as an essentially artificial but wholly necessary restraint upon the species' natural tendency towards mutual hostility, would be acceptable straightforwardly to Ferguson and his generally far-more-optimistic colleagues in the mid-eighteenth century. But the challenge posed by Hobbes's grim pessimism, as well as the remarkable ingenuity with which he had constructed his argument, was inevitably a powerful stimulus to Enlightenment speculation about the origins of society and government.

A much more favourable response would be reserved in the eighteenth century for the contribution of a second English thinker, whose ideological inclinations were, fortunately, quite different from those of Hobbes. John Locke, whose *Two Treatises of Government* (1690) eventually came to be regarded as a foundation-text both of the Enlightenment and of the American Revolution, offers another compelling account of the early development of human society. But this time it is clearly also a thinly-veiled attack upon what good Whigs considered the authoritarian and unaccountable exercise of late Stuart kingship, in opposition to which Locke had himself been much involved in the early 1680s. Locke's version of the state of nature, and thus the contemporary political lessons that could be drawn from how it had come to an end, contrasts starkly with that of Hobbes. For in Locke's view, whilst society was indeed first formed by a contract between men, this time it was conceived as a mutual agreement which was, crucially, binding upon rulers as well as upon the ruled. Moreover, such a reciprocal arrangement had only arisen in the first place, according to Locke, because people had needed effective institutions with which to preserve their own persons and properties—their 'life, liberty, and estate', in the Englishman's much-quoted words (TTG, 323). By a momentous deduction, it followed that, if political authority had only been created so as to protect those rights, any subsequent government failing in this fundamental duty must not only forfeit any claim to continued legitimacy but can also be removed by the express will of the people. As will be clear, Locke's theory of society, once more buttressed with historical evidence ranging from modern Europe to the tribal peoples of the North American woodlands, therefore appeared to his doting eighteenth-century readers to supply a decisive argument in favour of just that kind of responsible representative government, liberal parliamentary monarchy and consistent rule of law which, as supposedly guaranteed by the Revolution of 1690, was increasingly viewed as the distinctive birthright of the Scottish and English political elites.

Yet if we wish fully to understand the diverse intellectual threads which finally converged in the person of Adam Ferguson in the middle years of the eighteenth century, we cannot afford to ignore the means by which these erudite discussions elsewhere in Britain and Europe about the origins and nature of human society eventually came to be so familiar to educated men in post-Union Scotland. For there are strong indications

that, at least by the last years of the seventeenth century, Scottish culture too was increasingly feeling the impact of the most powerful and
most vigorous philosophical currents in foreign parts. Viscount Stair,
for example, published his *Institutions of the Laws of Scotland* in 1681,
an unprecedented attempt at the systematic rationalisation of Scots law
which imported the insights of Grotius and his Prussian disciple Samuel
Pufendorf so as to help explain and expound his own country's peculiar
legal heritage. Moreover, around the same time the Scottish universities
were also beginning to reveal a precocious openness to new ideas. These
included the scientific teachings of Sir Isaac Newton and the medical doctrines of Hermann Boerhaave: together these would soon help establish
Scotland's reputation in what would become key areas of Enlightenment
education. Simultaneously there is evidence that, at the turn of the eighteenth century, university academics in Edinburgh, Glasgow, St Andrews
and Aberdeen were eagerly incorporating the theories of the Continental
natural lawyers, with all their suggestive hints and fertile suggestions
about the possible origins of human society: Pufendorf, for example,
became a standard philosophical textbook at Glasgow under the supervision of the great Gershom Carmichael, himself the inspiration and predecessor of Hutcheson. As Dugald Stewart would later observe, it would
turn out to have been absolutely crucial to the subsequent flowering
of the Scottish Enlightenment that Grotius and Pufendorf had thereby
'made their way into the Universities' (DEGV I:53).

It is clear, moreover, that the Scots' own growing interest in the history
of society during the first half of the eighteenth century was also being
influenced by even more recent intellectual developments. Perhaps most
crucially, it was their unbounded admiration for the works of Charles-
Louis de Secondat, Baron de Montesquieu, the leading philosopher of
the early French Enlightenment and a man whom they believed had
opened up entirely new perspectives on the human condition, that seems
particularly to have excited Scottish theorists by the 1750s. Indeed, of all
modern writers, Montesquieu enjoyed an unsurpassed reputation among
the Scots—'That justly celebrated author' according to Lord Kames, 'the
immortal Montesquieu' in the words of the Aberdeen historian John
Adams (SHM I:31; CT A2r). His painstaking accumulation of pertinent
historical examples and undoubted brilliance in conjecturing plausible
connections between seemingly disparate pieces of evidence, techniques
anticipated in the works of Bodin and Grotius but taken to new heights
in Montesquieu's *The Spirit of the Laws* (1748), even suggested to some

of his most ardent Scottish admirers that the recent achievements of the mathematicians and cosmologists might yet be emulated by those who aspired to understand man's experiences. But his specific conclusions about the impossibility of conceiving of man divorced from his social context, and about the need to explain the development of humanity in terms of a set of interacting psychological and environmental causes, were also hugely important to Scotland's own emerging social theorists. Certainly they were acknowledged as representing the cutting edge of current thinking on this problem and so the obvious starting-point for Scottish inquiries: as Ferguson himself noted approvingly in the first pages of his *Essay*, his deference to the great Frenchman almost palpable, "'Man is born in society'", says Montesquieu, "'and there he remains'" (E 21).

At the same time it is evident that continual local reinforcement of this range of prior influences from outside the country was crucial in shaping the approach of Ferguson and his Scottish contemporaries to the investigation of society's origins. In this respect the key intermediary role was undoubtedly played by Hutcheson, ensconced in Glasgow from 1729 and, as we saw in Chapter 2, energetically propagating within Scotland a type of moral philosophy in which the leading English and European thinkers of the previous century provided the principal points of departure. It would be unwise, for example, to overlook the significance of natural law in Hutcheson's scheme, given his willingness to incorporate the jurists' trademark assumption—perhaps imbibed when reading Pufendorf in Carmichael's classes—that man was essentially a creature designed for society. Locke's empiricism was also the methodological baseline for Hutcheson's philosophical claims, as was his liberalism for the Glasgow professor's notably progressive political doctrines: in fact, in this regard, no eighteenth-century Scottish thinker was entirely untouched by Locke's ubiquitous influence. Nor, rather more provocatively, can Hobbes's glowering presence in the background be ignored: his intolerable insistence upon the primacy of individual self-interest was, after all, the main reason why Shaftesbury's arguments for man's innate capacity for moral judgment and benevolent action had been borrowed and disseminated so influentially by Hutcheson. Transmitted not only directly to his Glasgow students, but also to a wider public through the pages of the *Enquiry into the Original of our Ideas of Beauty and Virtue* (1725) and *An Essay on the Nature and Conduct of the Passions and Affections* (1728), Hutcheson and his powerfully-argued philosophical system were probably the dominant intellectual influence in Scotland at mid-century. Certainly it is difficult to believe that, without him, the emerging Enlightenment, and the intensely fruitful preoccupation with the origins and nature of human society that provided such a central feature of Ferguson's career in particular, could have taken quite the form that they did.

ii

If the ambition of all eighteenth-century intellectuals was, in the familiar words of Alexander Pope's epigram, to demonstrate that 'the proper study of Mankind is Man', then the background that we have just sketched also ensured that the comprehensive investigation of human society in all its many guises would be accepted as the Scottish Enlightenment's most fundamental inquiry (EM 53). As Ferguson in turn explained this basic requirement to the curious readers of the *Essay* in its opening pages:

> Mankind are to be taken in groupes, as they have always subsisted. The history of the individual is but a detail of the sentiments and thoughts he has entertained in the view of his species: and every experiment relative to this subject should be made with entire societies, not with single men. (E 10)

This, then, is the essential justification for Ferguson's lifelong interest in the study of man as part of a wider community. For without it there can be no meaningful knowledge of man as a creature. Social settings, Ferguson insists here, provide the only possible context within which to extend our understanding of mankind, because, as the great philosophers of the seventeenth century had already conclusively established, most of the main features of the human condition are themselves an inescapable consequence of our social existence. Indeed, divorced from that environment—even supposing that such a state were even remotely conceivable—man, quite literally, would not be man.

Why, it was therefore necessary for Ferguson to go on to explain, had man always been such a definitively social creature? And why in practice was he invariably encountered not in isolation but among his family, his friends, his neighbours and his fellow-countrymen? Again Ferguson had an answer very much in keeping with what his eminent recent predecessors had taught him about the psychological construction of the human mind. For the key to explaining those unvarying social tendencies exhibited by all men in all times and places lay clearly in what Ferguson himself called 'certain instinctive propensities'—that is to say, a potent series of elementary human impulses which, to borrow Ferguson own words, 'lead him to perform many functions of nature relative to himself and to his fellow-creatures' (E 16). These instincts, moreover, or innate capacities, have a number of characteristic dimensions. As Ferguson continues to elaborate this fundamental point in the early pages of the *Essay*, almost as if consciously working outwards from Hobbes's insufferably narrow emphasis upon the instinct for self-preservation and towards the wider, more benign and more constructive human impulses which Locke and Montesquieu had subsequently chosen to stress:

He has one set of dispositions which refer to his animal preservation, and to the continuance of his race; another which lead to society, and by inlisting him on the side of one tribe or community, frequently engage him in war and contention with the rest of mankind.

In other words, a propensity for identifying and belonging to groups or communities exerts at least as powerful a pull upon our decision-making and behaviour as the desire for individual survival with which it is inextricably linked. Indeed, we are impelled by our very natures to act in accordance with its dictates. As James Grant, an Edinburgh advocate and antiquarian, put this same point rather more succinctly in his own *Essays on the Origin of Society* (1785)—the title of this work again emphasising the topicality and marketability of such concerns in Scotland during this period—man always seeks instinctively to gratify 'the social disposition of his kind' (EOS 3).

The absolutely central importance to Ferguson's social theory of this basic conception of man as instinctively social is further underlined by the fact that several other sections of the *Essay* actually turn out to advance much the same argument, and often on more than one occasion. In particular, Section III, tellingly titled 'Of the Principles of Union among Mankind', provides a more expansive version of Ferguson's claims about the necessarily gregarious nature of mankind. It also offers an even clearer statement of how this is grounded in a genuinely instinctive yearning for the experience of society. Ferguson acknowledges here that this is a topic as obscure as it is important. He also concedes that previous theorists— no names are volunteered, though he clearly has Hobbes and his various antagonists in mind—have differed widely in their interpretation of the same evidence, especially in relation to how the very earliest stages of human history must have looked: 'The state of nature is a state of war or of amity', Ferguson recounts, 'and men are made to unite from a principle of affection, or from a principle of fear, as is most suitable to the system of different writers' (E 21). Intellectual dissension on this point, however, is not in itself a major problem. For disagreement over man's specific motivation for social engagement in a variety of circumstances is nothing more than further evidence for its sheer ubiquity in his psychological composition: in other words, at least by Ferguson's reckoning, the disputes between theorists on the details merely confirm that, in general terms, a desire for membership of society is indeed rooted in man's very nature. Certainly this was a conclusion that Ferguson was right to imply had come to be accepted by most of the Enlightenment's earlier writers, even as they continued to differ, sometimes spectacularly, on the technical implications: 'Man, by his nature, is fitted for society, and society is fitted for man by its manifold conveniences', as Kames had expressed this belief; 'Nature has made men fit for society, and it has made society necessary for them', had argued Duncan Forbes of Culloden, the distinguished Edinburgh judge and political administrator, in almost exactly the same words (HLT I:124; TRNR 9).

Having drawn attention to a largely unremarked but apparently illuminating consensus among otherwise very different writers, Ferguson is able to go on in the *Essay* to present the instinct towards society, and man's continual interest in his social environment, as a universal characteristic with any number of variant expressions—whether a pious concern for familial duties, mere slavish adherence to the multitude, or even a hankering after human contact of any kind when temporarily marooned in splendid isolation:

The charms that detain him are known to be manifold. We may reckon the parental affection, which, instead of deserting the adult, as among the brutes, embraces more closely, as it becomes mixed with esteem, and the memory of its early effects; together with a propensity common to man and other animals, to mix with the herd, and, without reflection, to follow the croud of his species. What this propensity was in the first moment of its operation, we know not; but with men accustomed to company, its enjoyments and disappointments are reckoned among the principal pleasures or pains of human life. Sadness and melancholy are connected with solitude; gladness and pleasure with the concourse of men. The track of a Laplander on the snowy shore, gives joy to the lonely mariner; and the mute signs of cordiality and kindness which are made to him, awaken the memory of pleasures which he felt in society.

In other words, by skilfully weaving together the disparate claims of his predecessors about the natural endowments of mankind, Ferguson is ultimately able to present with great power and conviction what is his own central proposition: that the human being is at once both similar to and quite different from other species. Man, he says, is able to feel a noble attachment to family and kindred, and to do so more keenly and with far greater enjoyment than other creatures, when he is guided by the full range of moral and prudential considerations to which he is subject. Yet at the same time, man also shows himself capable of mirroring the behaviour of unreflective animals, who instinctively flock and herd together even when guided by nothing more than natural impulse and force of habit.

iii

If society must therefore be understood as the natural and inevitable expression of a universal human propensity, then virtually all of Ferguson's other arguments in the *Essay* about the social consequences of human nature are able to rest on the securest of psychological foundations. This is not to suggest, however, that his subsequent account of man's development as a species is simply Ferguson's unconsidered recitation, or even just a particularly skillful re-packaging, of the familiar claims of earlier theorists like Grotius and Montesquieu. Indeed, in keeping with Ferguson's considerable delight in the business of debate and disputation—we need to keep in mind that it was a naturally combative temperament as much as keenly-felt principles that led him to participate so energetically in the disputes over the Scottish militia, *Douglas*, Ossian and the American and French Revolutions—his handling of what in the *Principles* he later aptly described as 'the much agitated question relating to the state of nature' needs to be interpreted as a frontal attack, executed with the dexterity of a habitual controversialist, upon several of the leading authorities who had previously treated this key problem in modern social theory (P I:27).

Both Hobbes and Locke in particular, it will be remembered, had painted the state of nature as a distinct phase in the early evolution of the species, albeit characterised in very different ways—in the former distinctly unpleasant, in the other rather more neutral. In both cases, however, it was implied that this had been an original condition from which mankind had eventually contrived to progress. A similar natural state, historically-concrete though long since abandoned, was implicit too in by far the most important recent contribution to this debate, that made by the Swiss philosopher Jean-Jacques Rousseau, first in the *Discourse on the Origins of Inequality* (1755) and then in his celebrated tract *On the Social Contract* (1762). The latter work especially was to become a landmark text of the mature Enlightenment, indelibly associated even today with the claim, resonating with its author's passionate dislike for what he believed had been unjustly imposed upon people since their departure from an almost Edenic state of nature, that 'man was born free, but everywhere he is in chains' (DCS 103). It was against the implications of this seminal theoretical conjecture—that the state of nature, in other words, was a pristine and primitive historical condition which, by finally entering into complex social and political relations, man had definitively left behind—that Ferguson launched one of the most rhetorically-charged and intellectually-significant assaults in the entire eighteenth-century European debate about the origins of society.

In the *Essay* it becomes clear almost immediately, in the opening section of the book, that in Ferguson's opinion, the evidence against believing that there ever had been one definitively natural state of human existence, particularly of a pre-social kind, is simply overwhelming. As he explains to us on the very first page, in beginning a section with the bald title 'Of the Question relating to the State of Nature', this assumption had become deeply-entrenched, seemingly establishing itself by the middle years of the eighteenth century as an integral part of some of the most widely-credited accounts of man's history as a species:

Not only the individual advances from infancy to manhood, but the species itself from rudeness to civilization. Hence the supposed departure of mankind from the state of their nature; hence our conjectures and different opinions of what man must have been in the first age of his being. The poet, the historian, and the moralist, frequently allude to this ancient time; and under the emblems of gold, or of iron, represent a condition, and a manner of life, from which mankind have either degenerated, or on which they have greatly improved. On either supposition, the first state of our nature must have borne no resemblance to what men have exhibited in any subsequent period; historical monuments, even of the earliest date, are to be considered as novelties; and the most common establishments of human society are to be classed among the incroachments which fraud, oppression, or a busy invention, have made upon the reign of nature, by which the chief of our grievances or blessings were equally with-held. (E 7)

As should be obvious from the insistent repetition of the words 'supposed' and 'supposition', however, Ferguson is in fact signalling to his own readers that what follows will not be a wholly deferential treatment of his predecessors' familiar claims. On the contrary, no well-informed contemporary, encountering this sweeping opening passage for the first time, and knowing everything that had already been written on this perplexing subject, could have been in any doubt as to the intensely polemical purpose of Ferguson's discussion of the state of nature, or indeed as to the specific earlier theorists whose arguments he was about to confront.

As Ferguson's discussion of this problem takes shape in the *Essay*, no individual state of nature theorist, among those 'who have attempted to distinguish, in the human character, its original qualities, and to point out the limits between nature and art', is actually singled out for explicit blame. But it is clear that he has certain writers very much in mind when he goes on to claim that 'some have represented mankind in their first condition, as possessed of mere animal sensibility, without any exercise of the faculties that render them superior to the brutes, without any political union, without any means of explaining their sentiments....' (E 8). Hobbes is presumably still the unnamed target of Ferguson's next piece of raillery: 'Others have made the state of nature to consist in perpetual wars, kindled by competition for dominion and interest, where every individual had a separate quarrel with his kind, and where the presence of a fellow-creature was the signal of battle' (E 8). According to Ferguson, however, such characterisations, all of them recognisably variations on the same doleful theme, have always failed the most basic of tests. For they rest on no direct observation and no credible evidence of that which they purport to describe. Indeed, if the duty of the 'natural historian' is, as Ferguson emphatically insists that it is, 'to collect facts, not to offer conjectures', and so to avoid the methodological solecism which imprudently 'substitutes hypothesis instead of reality', then no previous treatment of the state of nature can actually be considered remotely adequate.

Having precisely identified this fatal weakness in some of the most influential existing theories, it is necessary, according to Ferguson, for us to look in a rather different direction for plausible answers to the key questions that we wish to ask about man's natural state. Indeed, rather

than believing, without any corroborating evidence, that a pre-social
or pre-communal state of nature ever existed, Ferguson insists that we
should instead look to found our understanding of man's early development exclusively upon that which can be seen and evaluated in the historical record. And in this connection, it is no surprise to find Ferguson
arguing that the appropriate evidence runs very much contrary to the
ill-founded speculations of previous theorists:

> If both the earliest and the latest accounts collected from every quarter of the
> earth, represent mankind as assembled in troops and companies; and the indi-
> vidual always joined by affection to one party, while he is possibly opposed by
> another; employed in the exercise of recollection and foresight; inclined to com-
> municate his own sentiments, and to be made acquainted with those of others;
> these facts must be admitted as the foundation of all our reasoning relative to
> man. (E 9)

In other words, mankind is by his nature, and has always been, a social
creature; and it follows, in happy accordance with every available scrap
of documentary and observational evidence that we have received about
each distinct people in every known state and situation, that society has
been from the very beginning the only context in which men are likely
to be encountered. As will be clear, however, Ferguson's adept re-writing
of the natural history of human society entails an attack not only upon
the conclusions but also upon the analytical concepts utilised by earlier
theorists. For if a truly pre-social condition has never really existed, then
is it not necessary for us also to accept that man's natural state—the 'state
of nature' in its only meaningful sense—is simply each and every one of
those social situations, in all their near-infinite variety, in which he is
found in our own time?

Ferguson certainly appears to want his readers to embrace this critical
semantic shift in the philosophical debate. Indeed, targeting in particular Rousseau's visionary account of a lost paradise, he argues that the
'state of nature', in so far as it has any remaining value for the description
of mankind's history, needs to be understood not as a term connoting
a primitive condition which has been abandoned but rather as a phrase
applicable equally to every setting in which man is, ever has been, or will
be found. In fact, Ferguson's pronounced sensitivity to the extraordinary diversity of human social environments—a feature of his approach
which it is difficult not to relate in some way to his unusual personal
experiences as an Edinburgh academic who was also familiar both with

modern military life and with Gaelic-speaking rural society—greatly strengthens his critique at this point. For it reinforces his conviction that something is 'natural' precisely because it can be shown to be simply one among very many possible expressions or reflections of man's universal nature. The truly natural must necessarily be universal rather than particular. Indeed, it is a quality possessed by man's common experiences in all ages and places. Literally by definition, according to Ferguson's ingenious re-casting of the discussion, it cannot meaningfully be confined to specific—let alone entirely suppositious—conditions that could clearly only have obtained under exceptionally rare (and, as it turns out, wholly unverifiable) historical conditions.

The importance of pressing home this argument about the sheer ubiquity of our natural state is such that it also provides the occasion for more of Ferguson's formidably fluent rhetoric. In effect, this embodies Ferguson's determination to sweep away any alternative or narrower conceptions of what is actually natural to man, by offering his readers a veritable flood of authoritative generalisations about the rich variety of man's perfectly ordinary—or, as we might still want to say, natural—circumstances:

Man finds his lodgment alike in the cave, the cottage, and the palace; and his subsistence equally in the woods, in the dairy, or the farm. He assumes distinctions of titles, equipage, and dress; he devises regular systems of government, and a complicated body of laws: or, naked in the woods, has no badge of superiority but the strength of his limbs and the sagacity of his mind; no rule of conduct but choice; no tie with his fellow-creatures but affection, the love of company, and the desire of safety. Capable of a great variety of arts, yet dependent on none in particular for the preservation of his being; to whatever length he has carried his artifice, there he seems to enjoy the conveniences that suit his nature, and to have found the condition to which he is destined. The tree which an American, on the banks of the Oroonoko, has chosen to climb for the retreat, and the lodgement of his family, is to him a convenient dwelling. The sopha, the vaulted dome, and the colonade, do not more effectually content their native inhabitant. (E 13–14)

Having projected this compelling vision of man's limitless versatility and ingenuity, in many ways a classic articulation of the Enlightenment's characteristic faith in human adaptibility as well as of a growing willingness by the 1760s to entertain judgments of different societies that increasingly verged on explicit cultural relativism, it was, of course, that much easier for Ferguson now to interject his own blunt answer to the hoary old question:

> If we are asked therefore, Where the state of nature is to be found? we may answer, It is here; and it matters not whether we are understood to speak in the island of Great Britain, at the Cape of Good Hope, or the Straits of Magellan. While this active being is in the train of employing his talents, and of operating on the subjects around him, all situations are equally natural. (E 14)

By such means the claims and speculations of virtually all of Ferguson's major predecessors—optimists, pessimists, and fantasists alike—had been dealt a mighty blow.

Intimately related to this powerful emphasis upon the unrecognised universality of man's genuinely natural state, however, is Ferguson's suggestion that the word 'art', another term much-loved by eighteenth-century commentators, has been almost as mischievously deployed as the word 'natural'. For just as what is truly natural is actually far more extensive and much more varied in reality than the conventional conception of a lost state of nature had allowed, so that which might be deemed to be art—which is to say, to be artificial, synthetic, or man-made—is in fact equally extensive. Ferguson argues, indeed, that they are not to be understood as narrowly-defined antonyms, as the predatory accounts of Rousseau and many other thinkers had tacitly asserted. According to Ferguson, art and nature are in fact linked and over-lapping conceptions, which might even, in some circumstances, turn out, because of man's complex construction, to be effectively coterminous. As Ferguson makes this crucial further point, which obviously has profound philosophical as well as linguistic ramifications within the eighteenth-century debate about man's place in his environment: 'We speak of art as distinguished from nature; but art itself is natural to man' (E 12).

The consequences of embracing Ferguson's re-definition of some of the key terms customarily employed in arguments about the history of mankind are, as will be clear, as momentous as they are numerous. For we would find ourselves obliged to concede that many things previously thought of as being unnatural—in the sense that they are demonstrably the result of man's fabrication—might in fact have to be accepted as natural after all. Indeed, this line of reasoning is what eventually allows Ferguson to propose that man himself, as distinct from all the other species around him, should be understood as naturally an artful creature:

'He is in some measure the artificer of his own frame, as well as his fortune', Ferguson suggests, 'and is destined, from the first age of his being, to invent and contrive' (E 12). Small wonder, too, that Ferguson is keen to round off this discussion with a provocative summary of the argument which intentionally places in serious doubt whether we should even be willing to take at face-value the basic vocabularies, let alone the substantive interpretations, of his principal adversaries: 'Of all the terms that we employ in treating of human affairs', Ferguson concludes, 'those of natural and unnatural are the least determinate in their meaning' (E 15).

An only marginally less subversive feature of Ferguson's aggressive recasting of the existing discussion of man's natural state, however, is also worthy of consideration. For it confirms the extent to which his handling of this complex subject can be interpreted as part of an extended conversation with Montesquieu, Hume and other recent writers. Most importantly, it will be evident that in so strongly emphasising the formative impact upon his social surroundings of man's universal biological and psychological traits, there arises a special obligation for the theorist to provide a plausible explanation for the very obvious variations between the different customs and institutions that in practice result. In the case of Ferguson as much as that of his great French predecessor—though, significantly, not for Hume—climate and other environmental factors are what meet this need in a manner that is also pleasingly consistent with the tacit requirement for a fully naturalistic explanation of human existence. Thus some of the basic aspects of our lives are attributed by Ferguson to the uneven and inconsistent influence of our environment in different times and places: 'The circumstances of the soil, and the climate', he tells us in the *Essay*, when discussing the development of the earliest societies, 'determine whether the inhabitant shall apply himself chiefly to agriculture or pasture; whether he shall fix his residence, or be moving continually about with all his possessions' (E 96). As he pithily re-words much the same argument in the *Institutes*, again clearly siding with Montesquieu against his friend Hume: 'Men being dispersed over the face of the earth, receive the influences of climate, situation, and soil' (I 17). Societies, in other words, must inevitably differ in all sorts of detailed respects simply on the basis of where and in what physical conditions they happen to arise.

Even more obviously, in Part III, section I of the *Essay*, under the conspicuously Montesquiean title 'Of the Influences of Climate and

Situation', Ferguson expands this characteristically vigorous intervention in a pre-existing controversy, sketching for his own readers a strongly-contrasting picture of mankind's experience of relative advancement and development in the different climatic zones. Understandably, he seeks to reassure them, lest they doubt his continuing commitment to the universality of human nature, that man remains, at bottom, 'qualified to subsist in every climate. He reigns with the lion and the tyger under the equatorial heats of the sun, or he associates with the bear and the rain-deer beyond the polar circle' (E 106). But, no less than Montesquieu, Ferguson is also eager to emphasise the great variations in opportunity and achievement provided for different groups of humans by their particular climate. It is for this reason that he highlights the advantages that living in a temperate zone—not coincidentally home to what Ferguson thinks have been the most advanced civilizations in history—has conferred upon certain societies, as well as the contrasting disadvantages brought by proximity either to the Equator or to the polar regions: 'under the extremes of heat or of cold', he warns, 'the active range of the soul appears to be limited':

In the one extreme, they are dull and slow, moderate in their desires, regular and pacific in their manner of life; in the other they are feverish in their passions, weak in their judgements, and addicted by temperament to animal pleasure. In both the heart is mercenary, and makes important concessions for childish bribes: in both the spirit is prepared for servitude: in the one it is subdued by fear of the future; in the other it is not roused even by its sense of the present. (E 110)

The environment, in other words, affects in fundamental ways how human psychology will display itself, just as surely as it impacts upon other elements of our construction. These effects will even differ as to whether they are more or less desirable: for example, to be a naturally conquering people like the Romans or other 'nations of Europe', says Ferguson, and coming, by no accident, from 'happier climates', was very obviously preferable to being a society sunk in servility (E 110). All of these conditions, however, because only yet another manifestation of man's nature operating in combination with specific factors in his surroundings, are also to be understood as, in the final analysis, equally natural.

In choosing thus to present man's natural state as consisting not in some primeval condition of lost innocence but in an almost infinite variety of actual historical experiences shaped by the interaction of human nature and local conditions, Ferguson had clearly, with somewhat uncertain consequences, opened up new ways of conceptualising what we habitually call 'nature', and particularly, as we have already seen, about the language in terms of which the origins of society had come to be described by modern philosophers. Above all, if to refer to something as 'natural' is ordinarily understood as imputing to it a distinct moral quality—suggesting, according to context, that it is good, proper, normal, or acceptable—then Ferguson's dramatic widening of the term's potential application has unsettling implications for its continued employment as a judgmental tool. For example, might acceptance that what is natural is in fact everywhere around us, and that every widespread existing practice is merely an expression of our elemental humanity, require us to believe that everything that men commonly do is acceptable because it too is merely an authentic expression of their natures? In this respect it is surely not irrelevant that Hume, Ferguson's friend but also his most insightful philosophical critic, was perplexed by the tendency of too many thinkers to stumble into this yawning moral abyss. Indeed, Hume offers in the *Treatise of Human Nature* the typically barbed observation that it is a mistake to allow oneself to think that 'is, and is not' can automatically be conflated in discussion with an 'ought, or an ought not' (THN 469). Nor is it even clear that Ferguson himself, despite—or most likely because of—his primary duties as a moralist, had thoroughly faced up to this extraordinary consequence of his own, and the Enlightenment's, dalliance with cultural relativism: after all, this was a potentially bottomless chasm, necessarily fatal to all orthodox moral doctrines, into which he, like most of his colleagues, was simply unprepared to peer. One thing, however, was plain at the time, not only to Ferguson but also to his largely admiring readers. After 1767, the discussion of the state of nature—and thus the very foundation of conventional theories of society—had been changed forever.

iv

If, as we have seen, Ferguson wished to effect an important shift in the function of the state of nature within contemporary debates about society's development, he also remained concerned with emphasising the dramatic and dynamic processes by which the condition of human societies so often came to be transformed. Indeed, growth and not stasis, change rather than stability, were in Ferguson's opinion at the very heart of mankind's distinctive experience, as the openings words of the *Essay* make abundantly clear:

Natural productions are generally formed by degrees. Vegetables grow from a tender shoot, and animals from an infant state. The latter being destined to act, extend their operations as their powers increase; they exhibit a progress in what they perform, as well as in the faculties they acquire. This progress in the case of man is continued to a greater extent than in that of any other animal. Not only the individual advances from infancy to manhood, but the species itself from rudeness to civilization. (E 7)

Not surprisingly, therefore, the centrality of progress in Ferguson's account of man's history—by the time he published the Principles in 1792, 'Of Man's Progressive Nature' had become a largely uncontentious chapter title—was such that it went on to form clearly the dominant motif throughout the *Essay* (P I:189). And, in seeking once more to explain this universal feature of man's social experience by reference to what he believed were fundamental aspects of human nature, Ferguson also insisted that it was a yearning for material improvement in particular—a feature again found in previous theorists as different as Hobbes, Locke and Rousseau—which had made possible every other form of progress that man had achieved. As his friend Smith, whose philosophy would turn out to be rather more narrowly founded on this assertion, would summarise the same claim in *The Wealth of Nations*, a desire for betterment 'comes with us from the womb, and never leaves us till we go into the grave' (WN I:415).

Ferguson's ideas about the motivational power of material improvement are given a particularly extensive airing in Part II of the *Essay*, 'Of the History of Rude Nations', where, in section III, he describes how in even the most primitive or 'savage' conditions of society, such as those prevailing among the nomadic tribespeople of the Siberian wastes, acceptance of the concept of property ownership is already in evidence. For even in hunter-gathering communities, where most of the essential resources are effectively available at will to those who need to consume them, the notion of property has clearly taken root. It is, Ferguson says, 'already applied to different subjects; as the fur and the bow pertain to the individual, the cottage, with its furniture, are appropriated to the family' (E 95). Man's natural ambition and his prudent recognition that resources are not in fact infinite will, according to Ferguson, almost inevitably do the rest, ensuring an automatic trajectory in the general direction of progress and improvement: 'When the parent begins to desire a better provision for his children than is found under the promiscuous management of many copartners', Ferguson writes, 'when he has applied his labour and his skill apart, he aims at an exclusive possession, and seeks the property of the soil, as well as the use of its fruits'.

From this point onwards, man, 'urged as much by emulation and jealousy, as by the sense of necessity', is set on the road towards what on Ferguson's reading is emphatically to be understood as a perfectly natural process of change and development. Certainly it cannot be thought of as an insidious departure from man's true natural condition:

Thus mankind acquire industry by many and slow degrees. They are taught to regard their interest; they are taught to abstain from unlawful profits; they are secured in the possession of what they fairly obtain; and by these methods the habits of the labourer, the mechanic, and the trader, are gradually formed. (E 95)

Economic progress, in other words, is to be understood as the predictable consequence of man's inward instincts and his outward circumstances acting in fruitful concert. And from this the gradual development not only of more efficient technologies and productive systems but also of more elaborate customs, practices and social institutions can be traced: indeed, on Ferguson's reasoning, government, laws and forms of inheritance, as well as, ultimately, sophisticated commercial activity, all owe their origins to these same fundamentally natural human propensities.

According to Ferguson, an increase in warfare is, however, another of the natural corollaries of people starting to recognise more elaborate notions of property and ever-more numerous and varied possessions. Not only does this incline them to feud over questions of ownership ('the bands of society become less firm, and domestic disorders more frequent', observes Ferguson). For much the same reason, whole communities also engage in competitive activity, with the ultimate control of resources both the widely-recognised badge of honour and the immediate tangible objective: indeed, having successfully developed a clear sense of private property and so passed definitively from a 'savage' to a significantly more advanced (or, as Ferguson labels it, 'barbarous') state of society, characterised by settled farming and animal husbandry, 'Every nation is a band of robbers', he claims, exaggerating for effect, 'who prey without restraint, or remorse, on their neighbours' (E 97). In terms of the debate about man's nature in society, this means, of course, that warfare, and the material jealousies that lie behind it, cannot be dismissed simply as sterile and unproductive activities. Nor should they be portrayed as a regrettable deviation from the course intended for us by our very nature. In Ferguson's view, the violent pursuit of material gain is not only entirely natural. It is also the irresistible creative force behind many of the great revolutions and ruptures in our history: 'It was this spirit that brought our ancestors first into the provinces of the Roman empire', he chides those readers who may be squeamish about this argument, 'and that afterward, more perhaps than their reverence for the cross, led them to the East, to share with the Tartars in the spoils of the Saracen empire'.

Whilst the broader theme of man's relentless progress is clearly implicit in much of Ferguson's writing, he focuses upon it with particular concern for its moral implications in Part IV of the *Essay*, a famous discussion presented beneath the imposing title 'Of Consequences that result from the Advancement of Civil and Commercial Arts'. As this heading suggests, the emphasis here is again upon the material dimensions to human development. But now the conceptual core of the discussion, as well as the vital explanation as to how in practical terms economic progress is actually achieved, is found in what Ferguson chooses to describe, in the words of the title of section I, as 'the Separation of Arts and Professions'—in short, a phenomenon that well-read contemporaries will have noticed has strong similarities with that which Mandeville had first described at the turn of the eighteenth century as the 'division of labour', and which Smith, first in his Glasgow lectures in the 1750s and then later and hugely influentially in *The Wealth of Nations*, also considered extensively.

Consistent again with the empirical techniques developed by inspirational predecessors like Grotius and Locke, Ferguson's analysis is at this crucial point recommended to his readers not in speculative or in purely logical terms. Rather, it is presented as the only plausible deduction following actual observation of the historical evidence of functional specialisation spreading rampantly throughout society:

It is evident, that, however urged by a sense of necessity, and a desire of convenience, or favoured by any advantages of situation and policy, a people can make no great progress in cultivating the arts of life, until they have separated, and committed to different persons, the several tasks, which require a peculiar skill and attention. (E 172)

Ferguson is also adamant that specialisation has occurred because it makes clear economic sense. By encouraging dexterity and expertise, it makes a higher quality of production possible. For the same reasons, it also offers greater productivity and, as a direct consequence, improved profitability:

The artist finds, that the more he can confine his attention to a particular part of any work, his productions are the more perfect, and grow under his hands in the greater quantities. Every undertaker in manufacture finds, that the more he can subdivide the tasks of his workmen, and the more hands he can employ on separate articles, the more are his expences diminished, and his profits increased. The consumer too requires, in every kind of commodity, a workmanship more perfect than hands employed on a variety of subjects can produce; and the progress of commerce is but a continued subdivision of the mechanical arts. (E 172–3)

It is by these means that, as Ferguson triumphantly puts it, 'the sources of wealth are laid open; every species of material is wrought up to the greatest perfection, and every commodity is produced in the greatest abundance'. Progress, it is clear, is indeed a natural process, the 'result of instinct, directed by the variety of situations in which mankind are placed' (E 174). At the same time, it has impressive material manifestations which, at least in the economic sphere, appear to go far to explain the successful emergence and increased prosperity of commercial society itself.

v

Progress, however, particularly in the form of modern commercial society, remained for Ferguson very much a double-edged sword. It was undeniably responsible for many of the most important advances and improvements, particularly in man's material conditions and in the standard of living available to much of the population of modern western Europe. It had also ensured the gradual emergence of those sophisticated cultural practices, those elaborate social institutions and those highly-evolved political structures that distinguished an advanced and polished society such as the one in eighteenth-century Britain, in which, as we have seen, Ferguson himself was immensely proud to live. But was progress, especially in its economic manifestations, always such a good thing? Did it really make people happier or safer? And what were the drawbacks—even, dare it be said, the hidden dangers—of which his readers, blinded by the superficial attractions of wealth and plenty, also needed to be warned?

These critical perspectives were to be among Ferguson's most signifi-cant contributions as a social theorist, with wide-ranging implications also for an understanding of his place in the Scottish Enlightenment. For it is these arguments which above all tend to differentiate him from the markedly more optimistic judgments about man's development in society offered by Smith, Hume, and even Robertson. Indeed, Ferguson's much more equivocal analysis of human progress invites parallels with some of the less well-known, more classically-inspired Scottish thinkers of the eighteenth century—individuals like Thomas Blackwell, professor of Greek and subsequently Principal of Marischal College in Aberdeen, who in the 1730s had offered the distinctly ambivalent thought that 'the Manners of a People seldom stand still, but are either polishing or spoil-ing', or James Dunbar, regent of King's College, Aberdeen, who declared in 1782, even less promisingly, that 'Degeneracy as well as improvement is incident to man' (ELWH 14; EHM 1). Yet, as we shall see in Chapter 6, it was also precisely these more melancholy elements in Ferguson's social theory which ultimately provided those later admirers of his work who had their own reservations about commercial society with so much valuable food for thought.

Simply measuring the quantity of the *Essay* devoted to these much darker themes provides some indication of their relative importance. In fact, even leaving aside the numerous passing references to the problems brought by progress that litter the narrative as a whole, a full quarter of the text—comprising chiefly Part V with the title 'Of the Decline of Nations', and the concluding Part VI, called simply 'Of Corruption and Political Slavery'—is devoted specifically to what Ferguson himself called, in suitably philosophical language, 'the vicissitudes of human affairs'. But even as they give special force to the final sections of the *Essay*, the extent to which these concerns are woven closely into the fab-ric of his wider analysis of human society, and benefit from the same methods and modes of argument as the remainder of his account, needs to be appreciated: Ferguson's characteristic insistence upon the use of accumulated historical evidence, and his determination to explain all social phenomena in terms of the natural interaction of human psychology and the environment, are certainly present here no less than in his more pleasing discussions of men's universal instinct for community or their continual yearning for improvement.

As a result, in Ferguson's scheme the fact that societies can indeed experience decline—even perhaps extinction—emerges simply as the only plausible deduction from a host of familiar historical instances: it is therefore once again, at least as it is presented to the reader, a conclusion, however unnerving or uncomfortable, that it is remarkably difficult to avoid. The ancient contest between Rome and Carthage, to refer to one of Ferguson's favourite examples, had ensured that, whichever of the two rivals emerged victorious, 'a great nation was to fall' (E 197). Athens too, claims Ferguson, 'in the height of her ambition, and of her glory, received a fatal wound, in striving to extend her maritime power beyond the Greek seas'. But as well as these unhappy 'reverses of fortune', triggered directly by the malign interventions of powerful competitors, there have also been many examples of societies which have experienced what Ferguson calls 'a kind of spontaneous return to obscurity and weakness': of this less-easily-explicable kind of decline the Roman empire was itself the outstanding illustration, for, in succumbing to the depredations of the barbarian hordes, it had clearly been 'sunk at last before an artless and contemptible enemy' (E 198). At the same time, Ferguson's underlying assumptions about the differential rates of human progress attributable to the great variations in environmental conditions, which in turn encouraged him to imagine the existence of a natural pecking order of social advancement, obviously made it more difficult for him to explain convincingly how Rome's settled and highly sophisticated society—plainly superior in terms of its stage of development—could have been overthrown so completely by the undeniably more primitive Germanic tribespeople from beyond the Rhine. But he was convinced, typically, that the answer to this conundrum lay once more in universal tendencies of the human mind, and the way in which, in the more polished societies in particular, human nature might eventually cease to express itself in men's pursuit of the same noble objects as had inspired and strengthened their communities in less advanced situations.

'Improving nations', according to Ferguson, as he sketched out this sobering account of the latent potential for social decline, 'in the course of their advancement, have to struggle with foreign enemies'; they also 'enter on every new ground with expectation and joy: They engage in every enterprise with the ardour of men, who believe they are going to arrive at national felicity, and permanent glory...' (E 203). By the same token, less well-developed societies are naturally more vigorous and more energetic precisely because of the greater difficulties they face and the more substantial obstacles they need to overcome. In contrast, at least by Ferguson's reckoning, advanced societies, with their extensive size, complex institutions and widespread experience of ease and plenty, are fundamentally ill-suited to the cultivation of a population capable of continuing to appreciate, let alone to demonstrate, the loyalty, self-sacrifice, fortitude and endurance that their ancestors had once exhibited so successfully. One consequence of progress might therefore be that, in an important practical sense, its beneficiaries run an increased risk of losing their capacity to act with the vigour and determination necessary for their survival as a society:

A state of greater tranquillity hath many happy effects. But if nations pursue the plan of enlargement and pacification, till their members can no longer apprehend the common ties of society, nor be engaged by affection in the cause of their country, they must err on the opposite side, and by leaving too little to agitate the spirits of men, bring on ages of languor, if not of decay. (E 208)

The unfortunate results of such an internal state of affairs were evident, especially if an advanced society also happened to be confronted with a significant—it would no longer even need to be an overwhelming—external threat. In fact, it appears to be Ferguson's particularly troubling conclusion that, where progress, as often appears to have happened, encourages men 'to rely on their arts, instead of their virtues, and to mistake for an improvement of human nature, a mere accession of accommodation, or of riches', it renders their society especially vulnerable to decline (E 212).

It is therefore almost certain that Ferguson regarded progress towards a polished and commercial state ultimately with a substantially greater degree of ambivalence than most of his immediate Scottish circle. He considered that its attendant peace and stability frequently dulled some of the most active and beneficial impulses embedded in human nature—noble faculties that earlier times, precisely because characterised by austerity and strife, had once encouraged to shine forth. As Ferguson makes this point in another rhetorically-elevated summing-up:

We may, with good reason, congratulate our species on their having escaped from a state of barbarous disorder and violence, into a state of domestic peace and regular policy; when they have sheathed the dagger, and disarmed the animosities of civil contention; when the weapons with which they contend are the reasonings of the wise, and the tongue of the eloquent. But we cannot, meantime, help to regret, that they should ever proceed, in search of perfection, to place every branch of administration behind the counter, and come to employ, instead of the statesman and warrior, the mere clerk and accountant. (E 214)

In such carefully-constructed passages, Ferguson's concerns about the primarily economic forms in which man's progress tends to reveal itself are impossible to ignore, as are his consequent fears that modern societies remain peculiarly vulnerable to the threat of moral and political decline. A subsequent statement, the metaphor apt and the words resonating with anxiety, encapsulates perhaps the most important of the messages that Ferguson's original readers could have taken from the *Essay* in the late 1760s: 'The boasted refinements, then, of the polished age, are not divested of danger. They open a door, perhaps, to disaster, as wide and accessible as any of those they have shut' (E 219).

vi

Ferguson's theory of society, as we have seen, involved a complex and subtly-nuanced account of the natural development of mankind through history. In this often highly-distinctive analysis, progress, itself a consequence of man's universal nature, takes a number of different forms. It is connected in certain respects with material concerns, so that in this way Ferguson's treatment bears some relationship with the better-known theories of his friend Smith: it was implicit in Ferguson's system, for example, as we shall see in more detail in the next chapter, that hunter-gathering was succeeded by herding, and that farming was necessarily a less advanced form of subsistence than the modern system of international trade and commerce. At the same time, however, Ferguson had a moralist's concern for manners and behaviour, which proved at least as important for him in the characterisation of society's evolution. As a result, Ferguson's conception of progress also remained acutely sensitive to its potential reversibility—or, at least, to its failure to yield continuous improvement in all aspects of man's existence. These nagging doubts are particularly well expressed in the penultimate paragraph of the *History*, where Ferguson, having concluded his magisterial survey of the Roman republic, allows himself to offer a deeply pensive prospect of the fate that would in turn befall the Empire, for all its vaunted power and polish, in the fourth and fifth centuries:

As the spirit which gave rise to those forms was gradually spent, human nature fell into a retrograde motion, which the virtues of individuals could not suspend; and men, in the application of their faculties even to the ordinary purposes of life, suffered a slow and insensible, but almost continual decline. (H 481)

Ferguson's social theory, then, involved a conception of human progress that was ultimately very far from straightforward. And, as this distinctly gloomy interpretation of Roman history reveals, this was connected not least with his attitudes and assumptions as a student of the past. It is accordingly to Ferguson's activities as a historian that we should now turn.

Chapter Four

"Recollection and Foresight":
The Philosopher and the Historian

Adam Ferguson's career as a philosopher necessarily involved him deeply in the study of history. No naturalistic social theory could have been developed, and certainly no persuasive account of man's moral nature offered, without the fundamentally historical perspective within which Ferguson situated them. Principally this was because, as we have seen, working in Scotland during the second half of the eighteenth century, Ferguson was able to take it for granted—as could Smith, Hume and Robertson—that the most convincing evidence for human nature in all its complexity, and for the progressive development of man as a social creature, was available only through the systematic study of the past: as this emerging view had been expressed by Turnbull in 1742, it was clear that a 'very considerable acquaintance with history, and practice in drawing moral or political inferences from history is necessary.... seeing it is from facts or experiments that moral doctrines must be deduced, as well as physiological truths' (OLE 380). History, in other words, provided the theorists of the Scottish Enlightenment with an effective working laboratory—one which granted its skilled investigators access potentially to nothing less than the complete record of man's experience down the ages. It is likely that a naturally conservative political disposition may also have encouraged Ferguson in looking to previous ages as an inspiration for the present as well as for the future. But it is the scientific and philosophical methodologies underpinning the quest for a better understanding of the human condition, and which in turn led to an obsessive preoccupation with the accumulated evidence of society in all conceivable places and conditions, which best explain why Ferguson's keen imagination was so dramatically and so enduringly captured by the study of history.

i

In the same way as we have seen that close and conscious engagement with existing debates lent a powerful sense of direction to Ferguson's work as a social theorist and moral philosopher, so some appreciation of established traditions of historical writing—or historiography, as it is often called—helps us to understand how his interest in the past came to be nurtured and honed. In fact, in this respect it may well have been the immediately Scottish rather than the wider European background that exercised the greater formative influence. After all, as Hume famously observed of contemporary Scotland in 1771: 'This is the historical age, and this the historical nation' (HL 155). It would be mistaken, however, to see the nation's pre-eminent historiographical reputation as it existed during Ferguson's lifetime as wholly without precedent. For, since at least the era of the fourteenth-century wars against the English, in which the celebrated Declaration of Arbroath had deployed a resonant historical vision of their ancient independence to vindicate their country's cause before the court of world opinion, the Scots had been exceptionally adept at portraying themselves as a people defined above all by a shared past. John Mair and Hector Boece in the 1520s, and George Buchanan, the country's greatest Renaissance scholar, in the 1580s, had subsequently offered seminal histories of Scotland so as to make a series of contentious political points to their compatriots. And even the bitter religious disputes of the sixteenth and seventeenth centuries, in which the nation's Catholics, presbyterians and episcopalians had fought over control of church and state, were in an important sense merely a battle for the future ownership and use of a supposedly unique Scottish past. Could it finally be proved that the Scots, as John Knox and his reformist colleagues alleged, had always been an essentially Protestant people, though long oppressed by Popes and priests? Or had the Calvinist Reformation itself been only a late and illegitimate departure from native Scottish traditions of episcopal and/or Catholic piety?

Given this deeply-rooted national culture of historiographical activity and vigorous historically-grounded argument, it should not be entirely surprising that the Scottish Enlightenment, which, as we know, witnessed such a rapid expansion in authorship and publication within Scotland, also coincided with the country's recognition as perhaps the most important centre for the study of the past—indeed for other kinds of learned endeavour too—in the eighteenth-century world: 'The genius of the Scotch never shone with greater lustre than now', as Ferguson's other friend "Jupiter" Carlyle justifiably boasted in 1760 (QRSM 27). Certainly Hume's own masterwork, the *History of England* (1754–62), made him much richer and better-known in his own day, in France,

Germany and North America, as well as throughout Britain, than had his abstruse and far less accessible philosophical writings. The *History* was in fact among the most widely-read texts of the age, remaining a compulsory acquisition for any serious book-collector or library well into the next century. Whilst superficially purveying a consummately stylish and insightful account of English history, the razor-sharp political barbs and unmistakable subversive undertones embedded in Hume's masterly prose long proved capable of stimulating keen interest and heated argument among its innumerable readers

Another of Ferguson's close friends, William Robertson, who by the 1760s was technically his immediate superior as Principal at Edinburgh, had also matured into a historian of the very first rank: his *History of Scotland* (1759) was another best-seller, not least by virtue of its measured and notably humane treatment of the tumultuous era of the Scottish Reformation. But Robertson would soon add further bays to to his laurels—he was appointed Historiographer-Royal for Scotland in 1763—with new works of exceptional quality and public impact. First came the *History of the Reign of the Emperor Charles V* (1769), a majestic survey of sixteenth-century Europe as the crucible of the modern world, for whose copyright he netted what was then the staggering sum of £4,000. Following on from this literary (and pecuniary) triumph, and just as the American Revolution was stirring up unprecedented interest in the subject, there appeared the *History of America* (1777), the first part of a projected multi-volume study (the whole actually never emerging) in which Robertson explored with his readers the extraordinary pre-Columbian condition and dramatic early European settlement of the Americas. Finally, in 1791, Robertson published the *Historical Disquisition Concerning the Knowledge Which the Ancients Had of India*, which, beneath the slightly wordy title, provided a fluent and imaginative sketch of the fruitful relationship between Europe and southern Asia that had developed in antiquity.

Such works were, however, merely the outstanding landmark features within a broad and increasingly diverse historical terrain that, during the second half of the eighteenth century, appeared to many observers increasingly the collective property of Scottish writers in particular. One group who participated disproportionately in this remarkable outpouring of historiographical enthusiasm were the exceptionally characterful—in some cases, frankly eccentric—judges of the capital city, many of them Ferguson's friends and social intimates, who between them contributed a series of important and original studies that were widely read and admired, both at home and overseas. Kames's *Historical Law Tracts* (1758), for example, offered a series of thoughtful observations upon the evolution of law considered as a social artefact. The same author's *Sketches of the History of Man* (1774), his most popular historical work, widened the perspective to provide his readers with an elaborate account of the varied human experience of society. Lord Hailes, too, a kinsman of Stair, the celebrated jurist, was an extremely prolific writer, again specialising, not unexpectedly, in the study of legal history, but also compiling a number of well-received works in the fields of medieval Scottish history and ecclesiastical history—perhaps most famously the *Annals of Scotland* (1776), which comprised a close study of different episodes in the relatively-obscure period between the eleventh and the early fourteenth centuries. Lord Monboddo, meanwhile, yet another colourful extrovert on the Edinburgh bench, was a voluminous as well as quirky writer. He produced a six-volume dissertation *Of the Origin and Progress of Language* (1773–92), exploring the world's languages as a natural product of man's practical needs as a member of society, and *Antient Metaphysics* (1779–99), again in six parts, in which he speculated intelligently about the historical progress of the natural sciences and philosophy.

Other occupational groups closely involved in the Scottish Enlightenment, especially the university professoriate, the advocates and the clergy, also helped the country burnish its reputation both for the quality and for the variety of its historical literature. John Millar, Smith's talented pupil and for many years Glasgow's professor of civil law, published *An Historical View of the English Government* (1781), as well as a pioneering study in social structure, *The Origin of the Distinction of Ranks* (1771), which confirmed his reputation as one of Britain's most forward-looking and innovative historical thinkers. Hugo Arnot, advocate and antiquarian in Edinburgh, produced a hugely-popular *History of Edinburgh* (1779) in which the nation's and the city's stormy histories were skilfully interwoven—one of a number of urban, county or regional histories that appeared in Scotland after mid-century. Hailes's relation Sir John Dalrymple, meanwhile, yet another scholarly lawyer and kinsman of Stair, though at one time better known for having invented a process for making soap out of herrings, was responsible for the controversial *Memoirs of Great Britain and Ireland* (1771), whose review of the Revolution of 1689–90, an event still critical to the political and religious establishments of the later eighteenth century, provided contemporaries with ample scope for animated debate and disagreement. Even rural and small-town clergymen, like George Ridpath, a parish minister from Stitchell in Roxburghshire, and Lachlan Shaw, minister of Elgin, were not without their historical and antiquarian obsessions: the former's *Border History of Scotland and England* (1776) was another work which enjoyed significant contemporary currency, with its salacious but commercially-prudent emphasis upon the excessively turbulent past of his local region, whilst Shaw's *The History of the Province of Moray* (1775) reflected acutely upon changing social and cultural relations between Gaels and non-Gaels in Scotland's north-east.

A veritable craze for historiography, then, formed an integral part— and, at least quantified in terms of the numbers of books actually bought and read, probably the most extensive and influential part—of the broader intellectual culture of the Scottish Enlightenment. Strongly emphasising the value and the usefulness of studying the past in all its many guises, it profoundly influenced the cultural environment in which Ferguson's own philosophical career emerged and, indeed, without reference to which it would be unwise to think that we could fully comprehend his activities and concerns as a moralist and social theorist. But one further aspect of this rich local background also requires some preliminary comment. For the Scotland was already known by the end of the eighteenth century not only for the sheer scale (and, as we have seen, in some cases, the undoubted brilliance) of its contribution to the study of the past. It had also acquired a substantial reputation for an exciting new approach to historiography—a striking methodological departure which, though bearing some general resemblance to contemporary developments in France and in England, was in the particular form that it took distinctively and unambiguously Scottish.

Famously described by Dugald Stewart, in his flattering biographical account of Adam Smith, as '*Theoretical* or *Conjectural* history', though it has also come to be known simply as 'philosophical history', the broad features of this approach were and have remained relatively clear, despite much disagreement among recent scholars over the fine details (EPS 293). Above all, it is evident that philosophical history involved an attempt to transform the way in which the past was conceived and explored by modern scholars and their devoted readers. In particular, it was intended that they should be less preoccupied than previous generations were supposed to have been with compiling an accurate narrative account of individuals and events—which is to say, in disparaging terms, with history imagined merely as a leaden litany of reigns, statutes and battles. Philosophical history instead concerned itself with the self-evidently more important task of illuminating the psychological factors that had governed people's behaviour, as well as with the complex economic, social and cultural influences that had acted upon the evolution of particular institutions, practices and communities. To such an agenda, which necessarily implied that the historian should now investigate all manner of subjects not previously deemed worthy of study, we owe several of the endeavours already noted, such as Kames's ruminations on legal history and Monboddo's on language, as well as a number of other contemporary Scottish works whose very titles would have been inconceivable without the cardinal assumptions of philosophical history—for example, Dalrymple's *An Essay Towards a General History of Feudal Property* (1758), Smith's 'History of Astronomy' (published posthumously in the *Essays on Philosophical Subjects* (1795)), William Alexander's *History of Women* (1777), and John Macpherson's *Critical Dissertation on the Origin, Antiquities, Language, Government, Manners, and Religion of the Ancient Caledonians...* (1768).

Another obvious consequence of this marked shift of emphasis through the middle decades of the eighteenth century was that philosophical history, as was always intended by its Scottish exponents, proved especially well-adapted to the task of revealing the fundamental causes which lay behind the most momentous developments in the history of mankind: as this capability was explained to his own students in 1782 by Alexander Tytler, professor of history and one of Ferguson's younger colleagues at the University of Edinburgh, it was necessary to recognise 'the most important purposes of history, the tracing events to their causes, the detection of the springs of human actions, the display of the progress of society, and of the rise and fall of states and empires' (PO 5). As a result, it was anticipated that history would be able to shine unprecedented light upon the intricate operations of man's nature in all times and places: 'It is in the records of history, not in the conceits and abstractions of fancy and philosophy', insisted Gilbert Stuart, another Edinburgh historian though not a university professor, 'that human nature is to be studied' (VS Preface). In other words, and certainly not coincidentally, philosophical history was believed to be in a position to make a disproportionate contribution to the 'natural history of man'— in fact Stewart would add that 'natural history' had been yet another synonym for this whole approach—as well as to the wider "Science of Man" which formed the core enterprise of the Scottish Enlightenment. What this meant in practice for Ferguson, of course, was that several of the key works published from the 1750s, and which, not least being written by his immediate colleagues and friends, actually provided him with the greatest inspiration as a thinker and a writer, were themselves intimately concerned with the same dense nexus of psychological, social, economic, political and cultural themes in human history that, as we have already seen at some length, framed his own interests as a moral philosopher and social theorist.

This connection is perhaps especially evident in Robertson's writings, which, for all their undoubted fluency and easy charm, are sophisticated and far-reaching philosophical investigations in their own right. The *History of Scotland*, for example, provides a penetrating and unexpectedly sympathetic exploration of the character of Mary, Queen of Scots, suggesting—although not all of Robertson's contemporaries were yet ready to believe it—that she had been in many ways a sentimental heroine, the victim of cruel misfortune. *Charles V* is an even more remarkable venture. For, surely to the surprise of those readers led by its title to expect an orthodox political biography, it introduces the career of the eponymous hero with an ambitious analysis of Europe's social and political evolution in the thousand years between the fall of Rome and the era of the Reformation: in Robertson's persuasive re-interpretation, it is now factors such as alterations in property ownership, changing forms of social relations, shifting cultural preferences, and the gradual abandonment of older political values that largely explain the grand sweep of European history. Nor were such attempts at all-encompassing explanation confined to works which presented themselves explicitly as historiographical in nature. Indeed, it is probably fair to say that even that definitive foundation-text of classical political economy, Smith's *The Wealth of Nations*, with its characteristic interest in attempting to reconstruct the social and economic systems of earlier times, is not fully intelligible except as part of this wider fascination with untangling and scrutinising the disparate influences that have shaped man's development down the ages. Philosophical history, in short, was no peripheral development. Nor was it a mere literary fad. It was in fact nothing less than an integral part of the methodological foundations upon which came to be built the substantial intellectual achievements that we now know as the Scottish Enlightenment.

ii

It is clear, therefore, that Ferguson's concerns as a moral philosopher and
social theorist make substantially greater sense in the unique contemporary context created by the Scottish Enlightenment's intense preoccupation with historiographical study. Certainly Ferguson's treatment of history as a vast accumulation of evidence for human nature and the human
condition, although in important respects, as we have seen, a further
development from the inspiration provided by predecessors like Bodin
and Grotius, appears almost commonplace when set against this immediate Scottish background: none of his closest associates, for example,
would remotely have quibbled with Ferguson's insistence in the opening
paragraph of the *Principles* that 'In treating of Man, as a subject of history, we collect facts, and endeavour to conceive his nature as it actually
is, or has actually been...' (P I:1). Yet Ferguson's personal contribution to
Enlightenment historiography was not purely imitative and derivative.
Indeed, he was partly responsible, in collaboration with several of his
friends, for most of the innovations actually introduced during the most
productive and creative phase of philosophical history—which is to say,
between the 1760s and the 1780s. Ferguson did not, however, attempt
to intertwine theoretically-significant observations with a strong chron-
ological narrative: in fact, to show how far this mingling of new and old
techniques might be possible was very much Robertson's and Hume's
special contribution, and, in the event, an important reason for their
pre-eminent commercial success. Instead Ferguson, like Smith, sought
something even more ambitious: to develop inter-locking theories of
morality, society and politics which would be based squarely upon the
compelling testimony of human history. If these essentially non-narra-
tive priorities inevitably lead to the *Essay* in particular—as indeed they
also lead to the *The Wealth of Nations*—looking much less like a conventional work of history than does *Charles V* or the *History of England*, then
this is simply another measure of Ferguson's originality as an exponent
of philosophical history.

Beyond questions of overall investigative strategy and the unusual literary form that it turned out to require, however, Ferguson also made an
even more valuable and far-reaching contribution to the development
of history's theoretical or, as Stewart said, its 'conjectural' content. For,
in his quest for a plausible social theory that would explain how mankind had in some cases already completed the astonishing journey from

primitiveness to civilization, Ferguson created a sophisticated account of human evolution which embodied a number of critical assumptions about man's experience through history. To some extent this was about the very important technical matter of identifying the distinct phases through which communities actually passed as they progressed: for this problem Ferguson in fact had a number of interesting solutions which ultimately distinguished his work from Smith's—whose version has often been regarded as the definitive scheme. But Ferguson's desire for a naturalistic explanation of man's progress, linked with his commitment to the Enlightenment's trademark faith in the essential universality of human nature, was also to make him attempt some of the most imaginative and open-ended uses of philosophical history. Indeed, as we shall see, Ferguson's confidence in the underlying repetitiveness and uniformity of the human experience in all circumstances ultimately led him to entertain the possibility, at least in some restricted applications, that there might even be a predictive role for the historian.

In relation to the different stages through which human societies evolve, this question had had, like most of the others with which Ferguson's distinctive ideas were entangled, a particularly long and complex history of its own. 'Stadialism', a system which posits a series of separate developmental phases into one of which each society that has ever existed can be fitted, had deep classical roots, including in the writings of Aristotle himself. It had also received significant further consideration in the works of Grotius and Pufendorf which, as we know, form such an important part of the intellectual background to the Enlightenment in Scotland: as Stewart would later claim in his celebrated survey of European learning for the *Encyclopaedia Britannica*, there was a strong argument to be heard that it was in fact to the Dutch and German theorists of society, whose interests in the history of property had so influenced Smith's thinking in particular, that 'we are chiefly indebted for the modern science of Political Economy' (DEGV I:129). Yet the full flowering of stadialism, in the form of a group of closely-related explanatory models advanced by a number of scholars whose work was clearly known to one another, belongs very much to the third quarter of the eighteenth century, and to Scotland above all. Smith, for example, had been using his Glasgow lectures on jurisprudence (which is to say, the philosophy of law) during the 1750s and 1760s to develop the distinctive outlines of his own scheme: this encompassed four stages in the progress of mankind, each principally determined by the mode of economic production upon which its inhabitants depended for their subsistence, and by the characteristic notions that people entertained about the ownership and exploitation of property.

The first and earliest stage, described by Smith as that of 'hunting and fishing', lacked any concept of property at all, since all the material necessities of life were, at least in principle, available freely to everyone, as and when required. The second stage was 'pastoral', and, because it depended upon the domestication and rearing of herds, which were clearly a form of moveable property, it had also triggered the development of notions of ownership—representing, of course, a new and seminal form of abstract thought—as well as the rudimentary social institutions that were required to give them substance. By the third stage, the 'agricultural', an even more complicated social environment, marked by rules and laws relating to the ownership of land, had emerged: these were what had made it possible to manage all of the complexities implicit in the occupation and use of fixed forms of property by different groups. Finally, the 'commercial' state, in which Smith considered that modern Britons increasingly basked, was the most sophisticated (and demanding) of all: with its wealth ever more reliant upon complex trading networks and manufacturing systems, society by this stage had had to generate the full panoply of laws and institutions, as well as a high degree of functional specialisation, with which Smith's own students and readers, the inhabitants of a nation rapidly extending and diversifying its commercial and industrial activities, would themselves be increasingly familiar.

For his part, Ferguson's account of stadial development, of which the *Essay* was by far and away his most substantial exposition, was undeniably simpler than Smith's. At the same time, however, it is rather less easily described. Its simplicity consists not least in its offering a much terser sketch of human progress: in essence Ferguson presents us with just two early and one later stage of society, the first denominated 'savage', the second 'barbarous', with the third and final stage—clearly that in which Ferguson's eighteenth-century readers themselves are presumed to live—described variously (and usually without Ferguson bothering to explain the shifts in definitional focus) as 'polished', 'polite', 'civilized' or 'refined'. The distinction between 'savage' and 'barbarous', moreover, appears to operate in many ways like Smith's earlier stages of society, in that it rests primarily upon whether or not notions of private property have yet been called into existence. But it also becomes clear on closer inspection that Ferguson's scheme is by no means merely a condensed paraphrase of Smith's. In particular, Ferguson's 'barbarous' stage seems to comprehend both of Smith's two intermediate stages: whether fundamentally pastoral or agricultural societies in terms of their principal modes of production, Ferguson conceives of them both as belonging to a single amorphous category that supersedes man's existence as hunter-gatherer and is the precursor to his latter-day emergence as, in effect, a Glasgow tobacco merchant or Edinburgh advocate.

Nor is this the end of Ferguson's distinctiveness as a theorist of historical development. For it follows from his looser conception of stadialism that it cannot rest—at least anything like so much as Smith's clearly does—upon straightforwardly economic considerations. Indeed, whilst he accepts that, as he memorably says, 'property is a matter of progress', Ferguson's descriptions of the 'savage' and the 'barbarous' leave the reader little room for doubt that they are characterised by a wide variety of features which manifest themselves in a number of different ways (E 81). In some places, the distinguishing feature may well be the typical productive activity: this is, after all, what by definition separates the 'savage' from the 'barbarous'. But in other cases it is evidently a judgment about social organisation, or about cultural advancement, or about political institutions, ideas and values, or even, thinking very much as an Enlightenment moral philosopher, about characteristic forms of behaviour—'manners' in the jargon of the age—that he has in mind when assigning a society to a particular category. As a result of Ferguson's willingness to look beyond wealth and commerce, so far from his stadialism rendering him vulnerable to the charge of crude economic reductionism—as he explicitly warns in the *Essay*, we ought 'not to consider these articles as making the sum of national felicity, or the principal object of any state'—his analysis actually takes a much more pragmatic view of society's characteristics, offering us an account of human development which is never hostage to a single definition of progress (E 140).

It is also clear that, for Ferguson's work as a historian of mankind, this flexibility in his conception of stadialism has a number of specific consequences. One obvious corrollary is that, in happy concordance with widely-known historical evidence, the great variations in the speed and extent of progress between different human communities become more readily explicable: ultimately, with no iron law of social evolution at work, the exceptions and the difficult cases, always a major problem for those wedded to a rigid historical determinism (as some of Ferguson's less flexible disciples would later find), become correspondingly easier to account for. Indeed, Ferguson was especially keen to highlight the apparent anomalies, and, as we have seen, to demonstrate that, particularly by reason of their immediate environments, certain societies were actually better able to respond to the call of progress than others. A second advantage to the latitude with which he approached the categorisation of societies was that Ferguson was able to imbue his account of human development with a markedly greater degree of caution than had been either possible or desirable for Smith. His sensitivity to non-economic factors certainly made it more plausible for him to cast doubt upon the unvarying benevolence of progress, and to challenge those contemporary prophets who saw only advantage in the relentless march of commerce and politeness. As we have already seen in Chapter 3, moreover, this helped give his social theory a pronounced double-edge, even as it added to the predictive dimension of his writings a distinctive sense of foreboding about the future facing his modern readers. It also made it easier for Ferguson to set his own historical analysis alongside the markedly gloomy observations of colleagues like Arnot, Edinburgh's civic historian, on the future course of human progress: the latter even suggested in 1779 that men's manners develop towards 'an acmé of refinement, which degenerates into the basest corruption' (HE 51).

The conceptual elasticity of Ferguson's stadialism, however, also comes at a significant price. Above all, and as many critics have since noted, Ferguson's historical model, precisely because it is so hazily-defined at the margins, is deficient in hard explanatory terms. Indeed, it is a remarkable fact that the *Essay*, for all its ostensibly all-encompassing vision of man's natural history, offers its readers virtually no clear statement that would enable them to understand a society's eventual transition from one stage to another. Smith, by contrast, had provided a psychologically-plausible explanation of the ultimate limitations of one economic system in the judgment of men and its consequent replacement by a rather more congenial alternative. He had also added, consistent with an argument familiar from the natural law tradition, some further observations about the decisive pressure on resources applied by population growth. But Ferguson was able to say almost nothing that would shed new light upon why these critical transformations—effectively the great leaps forward in man's progress from 'rudeness' to 'civilization'—had occurred. Furthermore, the very vagueness of some of the most important definitions in Ferguson's hands makes the analytical integrity of his system potentially open to question. After all, if it is not particularly clear what precisely constitutes a 'polished' or a 'refined' society—and Ferguson certainly uses these labels relatively promiscuously at different points in his discussion—how coherent an account of the history of the species should we suppose that the *Essay*, for all its insistent scientific and philosophical rhetoric, is really offering? Nevertheless, as we shall see, the flaws in Ferguson's historical models, even as they provided useful ammunition for his detractors, did not substantially diminish what came to be widely seen by his contemporaries as the sheer scale of his achievement—or, for that matter, the reverence in which he was to be held by many of his long-posthumous readers. In fact, much the same was true of the other aspects of his contribution to philosophical history.

iii

Given what we have seen of the conjunction of several foundational assumptions among the philosophical historians of the Scottish Enlightenment, and particularly the effective fusion of these ideas in the work of Adam Ferguson, it is not difficult to explain two of the other central features of his analytical approach. One, which involved the belief that, in the absence of actual historical evidence, it was possible to use the general outlines of a stadial model to fill in the gaps, was of the very essence of 'conjectural' history: in a sense, the use of 'conjecture' turned the predictive potential of philosophical history in upon itself, proposing a credible method for reconstructing unknown events from the raw materials provided by what could be assumed to be equivalent historical conditions elsewhere in mankind's past. The other aspect of philosophical history to which Ferguson made a signal contribution is what is often described as the 'theory of unintended consequences'. Broadly sceptical about the ability of politicians or laws to deliver precise and foreseeable changes in the fundamental condition of society, this theory grew out of the interpretative claim that substantial change in history had demonstrably been the result of collective action at the social level, invariably unconscious—indeed instinctive—in nature, rather than the consequence of a small number of individuals acting deliberately and with those specific ends in view. Both of these approaches to thinking about historical explanation, linking Ferguson's interests in social theory, moral philosophy and politics with his study of the past, were also found in the work of his Scottish colleagues, notably Robertson and Smith. But again Ferguson's contribution was to be differentiated in a number of interesting and significant ways.

Ferguson's concern with the limitations but also with the possibilities of a 'conjectural' reconstruction of the past needs once again to be viewed in the context of one of his main polemical purposes, especially in the *Essay*. For in developing, as we have already seen, a sustained critique of Rousseau and the notion of a lost state of nature, he had ventured a number of strongly disparaging comments about the unwisdom of employing mere speculation in the writing of human history. As Ferguson observes of this danger, to which, he strongly implies, some recent students of mankind had been exceptionally prone:

...the natural historian thinks himself obliged to collect facts, not to offer conjectures. When he treats of any particular species of animals, he supposes, that their present dispositions and instincts are the same they originally had, and that their present manner of life is a continuance of their first destination. He admits, that his knowledge of the material system of the world consists in a collection of facts, or at most, in general tenets derived from particular observations and experiments. It is only in what relates to himself, and in matters the most important, and the most easily known, that he substitutes hypothesis instead of reality, and confounds the provinces of imagination and reason, of poetry and science. (E 8)

In Ferguson's view, grounded very much in the language of philosophical empiricism and in an unshakeable belief that the scientific method of observation and experimentation, validated above all by Newton's discoveries, was the model to be followed by those investigating mankind's natural history, the problem with conjecture, at least as employed by theorists like Rousseau, was that it seemed recklessly to detach itself from a proper regard for the evidence. Indeed, lost in what Ferguson elsewhere dismissed as 'the boundless regions of ignorance or conjecture', such theories, when subjected to the necessary tests, would inevitably fall at the first hurdle, compromised by their manifest inconsistency with demonstrable facts (E 12).

Nevertheless, in one specific usage, Ferguson's own analysis, especially in the *Essay*, remains clearly untroubled by the application of certain kinds of conjectural techniques to the work of the historian. In fact, when it comes to the very precise transplanting of relevant evidence and interpretation from a known to an unknown historical situation—at least where the principles of philosophical history confirm that the two circumstances are indeed closely comparable in developmental terms—Ferguson is perfectly comfortable. For example, in considering in Part II, section I, what he calls 'the History of Rude Nations', he remarks, with evident approval, that Thucydides, the Greek historian, had 'understood that it was in the customs of barbarous nations he was to study the more ancient manners of Greece' (E 80). In the next paragraph Ferguson goes further, suggesting that there is also considerable scope for conjecturing the lost early history of our own society. This opportunity exists precisely because we are blessed with a clear view of other peoples still locked in exactly that primitive state which we may suppose once imprisoned our own predecessors:

The Romans might have found an image of their own ancestors, in the representations they have given of ours: and if ever an Arab clan shall become a civilized nation, or any American tribe escape the poison which is administered by our traders of Europe, it may be from the relations of the present times, and the descriptions which are now given by travellers, that such a people, in after ages, may best collect the accounts of their origin. It is in their present condition, that we are to behold, as in a mirrour, the features of our own progenitors; and from thence we are to draw our conclusions with respect to the influences of situations, in which, we have reason to believe, our fathers were placed. (E 80)

Ferguson, then, fully endorses the use of 'conjecture' in the strict and technical sense familiar to his Scottish associates. It is permissible in circumstances where specific evidence is lacking but where appropriate information can be imported from a social setting which stadial models of social development show to have been historically-equivalent. Ultimately this is because, at least at the fundamental level—of concepts of property ownership, or of forms of social organisation, or of manners, for example—the universality of human nature means that the likelihood of achieving an acceptable approximation is surprisingly high.

Ferguson was in addition a willing exponent of the theory of 'unintended consequences'—or the theory of 'spontaneous order' or 'heterogeneity of ends', as others have since called it. It is true that the profile of this theory in Ferguson's Scottish circles had probably been raised significantly by its role in the problematical writings of Bernard Mandeville at the turn of the eighteenth century: these, as we have already seen, had given useful impetus to certain aspects of the Scottish Enlightenment's inquiries in moral theory and political economy. But Ferguson's particular comfort with the theory of unintended consequences is also partly explained simply by its fundamentally conservative ideological implications. For the theory proposes that those outcomes which comprise the more important parts of history—such as the invention of marriage, the first formation of governments, and the growth of commercial wealth— are the entirely unintentional product of men collectively following their natural instincts and interests. They are certainly not the consequence of individual statemen's wisdom, or even of the crowd consciously pursuing the radical designs of visionary leaders. As Smith famously argues in the *The Wealth of Nations*, even modern prosperity must therefore have essentially accidental origins, being the result of 'the private interests and prejudices of particular orders of men, without any regard to, or foresight of, their consequences upon the general welfare of society' (WN I: 3–4). Ferguson himself makes use of a similar argument at one point in the *Essay*, with a telling naturalistic metaphor designed to snuff out any thought that the grand sweep of history might somehow be determined by rational planning and decision-making: 'Like the winds, that come we know not whence, and blow whithersoever they list, the forms of society are derived from an obscure and distant origin; they arise, long before the date of philosophy, from the instincts, not from the speculations, of men' (E 119).

Ferguson, as we might again expect from his lifelong enjoyment of polemical activity, turned out to be one of the most eloquent and determined proponents of this politically-charged interpretation of historical change. Certainly he seized repeated opportunities to hammer home to his readers and his students the essentially unintended—and, indeed, unconscious—large-scale social consequences of our instinctive actions. In particular in Part III of the *Essay*, titled 'Of the History of Policy and the Arts' and dealing broadly with the role of culture and learning in human affairs, he persuasively asserts the historical significance of aggregate human activity, insisting that no deliberate intervention by a few wise individuals is capable of achieving as much as the blind instincts of the many:

Every step and every movement of the multitude, even in what are termed enlightened ages, are made with equal blindness to the future; and nations stumble upon establishments, which are indeed the result of human action, but not the execution of any human design. If Cromwell said, That a man never mounts higher, than when he knows not whither he is going; it may with more reason be affirmed of communities, that they admit of the greatest revolutions where no change is intended, and that the most refined politicians do not always know whither they are leading the state by their projects.(E 119)

Unintended consequences of this kind, of course, have innumerable implications for our understanding of man's past. Not least, we are obliged to approach with rather greater scepticism some of the conventional explanatory devices of narrative history. As Ferguson points out, once more instinctively turning for his example to the classical world with which he was on such intimate terms:

We are therefore to receive, with caution, the traditionary histories of ancient legislators, and founders of states. Their names have long been celebrated; their supposed plans have been admired; and what were probably the consequences of an early situation, is, in every instance, considered as an effect of design. (E 120)

In other words, for all the praise heaped upon figures like Lycurgus in Sparta, or Solon in Athens, or the early law-givers to whom the greatness of Rome has customarily been credited, philosophical history requires us to doubt—even as we also begin to better understand the causes of—the tendency of historians, as of poets and bards in earlier times, to ascribe the crucial causal agency to exceptional individual foresight. In reality, insists Ferguson, the rise of the most successful and most enduring city-states of antiquity was not the achievement of a series of uniquely-sapient founders. Rather, like just about everything else of real moment in history, it was merely the unplanned result of particular local circumstances and of the operation of certain natural tendencies common to the generality of men.

Ferguson's emphasis upon the unforeseen effects of our natural proclivities also allows him to account satisfactorily for many of the most significant events or processes in the history of the species (though interestingly not, as we have already seen, for the crucial transformative phase which interposes itself between the separate stages of a society's development). Like Smith, for example, Ferguson recognises that the division of labour—which is to say, the separation of economic functions between specialists—is an epochal development. For it is central to the growth of wealth which has come to characterise the more advanced stages of society. In Part IV of the *Essay*, titled 'Of Consequences that result from the Advancement of Civil and Commercial Arts', Ferguson offers a plausible analysis of the combination of natural factors which seem to have brought this situation about. As for Smith, who famously linked the division of labour with unintended consequences by describing it as 'the necessary, though very slow and gradual consequence of a certain propensity in human nature which has in view no such extensive utility' (WN I:16), what is most noteworthy in Ferguson's analysis of the phenomenon is the complete absence of any superintending wisdom or foresight:

> . . . The savage, or the barbarian, who must build and plant, and fabricate for himself, prefers, in the interval of great alarms and fatigues, the enjoyments of sloth to the improvement of his fortune: he is, perhaps, by the diversity of his wants, discouraged from industry; or, by his divided attention, prevented from acquiring skill in the management of any particular subject.
>
> The enjoyment of peace, however, and the prospect of being able to exchange one commodity for another, turns, by degrees, the hunter and the warrior into a tradesman and a merchant. The accidents which distribute the means of subsistence unequally, inclination, and favourable opportunities, assign the different occupations of men; and a sense of utility leads them, without end, to subdivide their professions. (E 172)

With an irresistible compound of unreflective instinct and healthy self-interest driving its innumerable individual members, society thus evolves new and more fruitful forms of economic organisation without any plan or obvious purposefulness. The truly seminal advances for mankind have clearly arisen, affirms Ferguson later, 'from successive improvements that were made, without any sense of their general effect; and they bring human affairs to a state of complication, which the greatest reach of capacity with which human nature was ever adorned, could not have projected' (E 174).

Given the overt ideological implications of this type of historical explanation, Ferguson's strong adherence to the theory of unintended consequences might also tell us something significant about his position in relation to some of the major public controversies of his lifetime. For such arguments can only have encouraged scepticism in the face of those late-eighteenth-century contemporaries who advocated radical change. We know, for example, that Ferguson refused to become involved in the constitutional reform movements in Britain during the 1780s and 1790s, notwithstanding his philosophical dissatisfaction, as a Lockeian thinker, with certain features of the existing political arrangements: as he wrote to his friend Sir John Macpherson in January 1780, it was particularly worrying to Ferguson that Yorkshire, a veritable hotbed of reform, was 'forming itself into a Republic', and that progressive country gentlemen there seemed eager to 'rise above all considerations of Reason, of Private Interest or of public Order' (C I:233). Instinctive caution in response to demands for radical political innovations would in fact be entirely consistent with Ferguson's approach as a philosophical historian. For it was precisely because long-evolving structures for the peaceful government of society, such as those Hanoverian Britain possessed, were actually the benign but unintended product of countless individual actions and decisions over the centuries, that they in truth required, at most, only further modest amendment at the hands of careful modern legislators.

These may also be the essentially conservative assumptions lying behind Ferguson's repudiation of the extravagant claims of the American revolutionaries, as seconded by Richard Price: in Ferguson's words in 1776, Roman history 'shows the danger of going so fast in search of ideal perfection, which is apt to make us despise what is attainable and obtained, for the sake of something impracticable, and sometimes absurd' (R 14). It is even possible that Ferguson's interest in the gradual and largely unintended character of large-scale historical change explains some of his remarkable ambivalence towards the French Revolution after 1789, to which we shall return in the next chapter. For, whilst acknowledging the grave military threat that France obviously posed in the eyes of all staunchly-patriotic Britons, Ferguson also seems to have had some sympathy for an argument, based on the theory of unintended consequences, that was most famously enunciated by the Irish politician and thinker Edmund Burke in his *Reflections on the Revolution in France* (1790): that the new-fangled and essentially speculative systems of government espoused by the revolutionary leadership would necessarily be inferior to the alternative, namely a piece-meal and sympathetic reform of the existing constitutional fabric which was itself the cumulative product of the natural instincts of numberless people down the ages.

Even so, it is worth noting that the consistently benevolent character of unintended consequences was also something about which Ferguson was far from confident. As we have seen, Ferguson often implied to his readers that unplanned outcomes—in other words, those arising incrementally from the natural impulses of the many rather than at one stroke from the grandiose and impractical flights of fancy of the few—were much to be preferred. Indeed, in an intriguing analysis of established political order in Part VI of the *Essay*, he hints strongly that a system of participatory government evolving gradually over centuries—presumably the Hanoverian parliamentary monarchy was specifically in his mind—is again convincing evidence of the invariable superiority of those structures and institutions delivered to us as unintended consequences:

> Men, in fact, while they pursue in society different objects, or separate views, procure a wide distribution of power, and by a species of chance, arrive at a posture for civil engagements, more favourable to human nature than what human wisdom could ever calmly devise. (E 255)

But by the same token, it is clear that Ferguson also had reservations about some changes of this magnitude. In fact, even in his analysis of the division of labour, in many ways a model exposition of the operation of unintended consequences in history and one which has obvious affinities with Smith's more famous employment of the concept in the *The Wealth of Nations*, there appear to be significant anxieties on Ferguson's part about the moral disadvantages of certain aspects of this phenomenon.

In particular, it is surely important that Ferguson chooses to discuss this primarily economic phenomenon in an especially thought-provoking section of the *Essay* which bears a potentially-unnerving title for the inhabitants of wealthy but perhaps complacent late eighteenth-century Britain: 'Of Relaxations in the National Spirit incident to Polished Nations'. Indeed, for all the material blessings undeniably poured down upon mankind by the perfectly natural process of economic specialisation, it was equally obvious to Ferguson that, in its more advanced form, the specialisation of occupations tended simultaneously to work against the interests of social cohesion:

> But apart from these considerations, the separation of professions, while it seems to promise improvement of skill, and is actually the cause why the productions of every art become more perfect as commerce advances; yet in its termination, and ultimate effects, serves, in some measure, to break the bands of society, to substitute form in place of ingenuity, and to withdraw individuals from the common scene of occupation, on which the sentiments of the heart, and the mind, are most happily employed. (E 206–7)

Nor was this all. For, as we noted in Chapter Three, Ferguson was also adamant that social polarisation, a pronounced feature of advanced societies, carries with it serious and plainly undesirable moral implications for the welfare—even for the survival—of society as a whole. As his emotive oration continues:

Under the *distinction* of callings, by which the members of polished society are separated from each other, every individual is supposed to possess his species of talent, or his peculiar skill, in which the others are confessedly ignorant; and society is made to consist of parts, of which none is animated with the spirit of society itself. (E 207)

Like Smith, therefore, Ferguson seems to have remained conscious of the essentially Janus-faced character of progress. On the one hand, men's instincts and interests ultimately brought about wealth and ease and plenty. The same natural propensities even helped create previously-unimaginable opportunities and wider horizons, which further enriched the lives of countless individuals. But on the other hand, the very operation of the division of labour—the self-same natural process by which, as Ferguson acknowledges, 'the sources of wealth are laid open'—had no less unintentionally achieved the disassociation or alienation of individuals from their communities, as men, once generalists with interests and values in common, now increasingly pursued only their own specialist occupations and individual requirements (E 173). In Ferguson's chilling words, which link the theory of unintended consequences directly back to his specific fear that advanced societies, despite their vaunted politeness, remain peculiarly susceptible to decline, it seems that one of the unforeseen implications of progress is that it might in fact make men so that they 'can no longer apprehend the common ties of society, nor be engaged by affection in the cause of their country' (E 208).

iv

This, then, was the greatest irony, even the potential tragedy, revealed by Ferguson's close study of historical explanation. Yet, as we have already seen, the essential ambiguity of human progress was just one of several aspects of Ferguson's involvement in historiography which begin to look somewhat different—and also, perhaps, rather more intelligible—when viewed in the highly-specific context of the Scottish Enlightenment. Most importantly, the function of history as empirical validation for Ferguson's remarkable theories about the natural evolution of society and about the double-edged implications of progress starts to come into sharper focus. So too does its role as a vehicle by which Ferguson was able to make a useful contribution to a multi-disciplinary public dialogue underway among and between his immediate Scottish friends—particularly Smith, Hume and Robertson. Indeed, more than almost anything else published in Scotland or in Britain at this time, Ferguson's writings, and the *Essay* above all, emerge as the embodiment of those conjoined interests in psychology, sociology, ethics and the study of the past that philosophical history, perhaps the Scottish Enlightenment's most important technical achievement, was all about. For historiography allowed Ferguson, like the natural man he described in a famous passage in the *Essay*, to immerse himself in that most instinctively human of activities, 'the exercise of recollection and foresight' (E 9). Nowhere, however, was Ferguson's interest in linking the past with the future to be more important than in framing his political philosophy. It is therefore finally his theory of government and, even more importantly, his theory of citizenship, that we need to consider.

Chapter Five

"Those Arts of Deliberation, Elocution, Policy, and War": The Political Philosopher

If one word encapsulates Adam Ferguson's political philosophy—though it certainly raises more interesting questions than it provides easy answers—it is 'Rome'. For the extraordinary history of this one city fascinated him from boyhood to old age. As a deeply-learned man situated at the heart of Scotland's enlightened intelligentsia, it allowed him to occupy common ground with the rest of his social circle, for whom a comprehensive grounding in classical history was an accepted foundation of their culture. As a professional teacher and writer, it also provided him with a vast fund of anecdote and story, and a cast of larger-than-life characters, with which to instruct and to entertain. But above all, it offered Ferguson, as a student of mankind, an unrivalled reservoir of information about human nature and the human condition during one of the most tumultuous and distinguished periods in history. Indeed, Rome, in little more than a thousand years, had even witnessed—or so Ferguson and his friends generally assumed—the complete progression of a single society from 'rudeness' to 'civilization', and then back again: as Ferguson told Edward Gibbon, a man with his own notable Roman fixations, in a revealing letter written in April 1776, 'I comfort myself that as my trade is the Study of human Nature I coud not fix on a more interesting Corner of it than the end of the Roman Republic' (C I:141). Yet Rome also had an even more immediate significance. For during Ferguson's lifetime, as perhaps the most familiar political metaphor of the age, Rome's rise, apotheosis and subsequent demise seemed to afford the inhabitants of mid-eighteenth-century Britain, and especially those of them who, like Ferguson himself, believed in the often repetitious nature of history, a salutary and uniquely well-documented lesson about the nature of their own government and its prospects for survival.

Following the Peace of Paris in 1763, George III, comprehensive victor over France in the recent worldwide wars, had emerged suddenly as the modern world's Caesar, the ruler of a vast and opulent empire extending from southern Asia to the eastern seaboard of North America. Yet deep anxieties, provoked by the multiplying problems of imperial

over-extension and by the seemingly irresistible temptations brought
by unprecedented British wealth and power, had almost immediately
begun to crowd in upon the minds of many of the king's classically-
trained subjects. The restive American colonists were already moving
towards open revolt, and then, finally, defiant independence. Powerful
foreign enemies were also circling watchfully, waiting for the moment
to launch a decisive counter-attack. And at home there was mounting
evidence of political factionalism, governmental dishonesty, and widespread moral laxity. Was it not therefore obvious that Britain was heading blindly in the same direction as Rome—towards a precipitous fall
into what Ferguson, not one to mince his words, would tell the readers
of his *History* had been nothing less than a 'ruinous abyss' (H 481)? In
these anxious and uncertain times, then, the complete intertwining of
Ferguson's political concerns and his abiding scholarly interest in the
study of what he memorably described to Gibbon as 'the Disstractions
that broke down the Roman Republic' greatly enhanced the relevance
of what he was trying to say as a historian and commentator (C I:141).
They also rendered his political philosophy unusually practical, even in
some instances immediately topical, in its implications.

i

Once again, it is necessary at the outset to say something of the specific
intellectual background against which Ferguson's ideas about government emerged from the 1750s onwards. For as much as the other aspects
of his writings, Ferguson's interests and aims as a political theorist were
largely formed in response to previous contributions and existing controversies in this field, which not only substantially defined the terms of
the debate but also provided Ferguson, always argumentative to a fault,
with much of his motivation. Not surprisingly, an important aspect of
the literary context to Ferguson's lifelong preoccupation with Roman
politics lies in the extensive scholarly, and especially historiographical,
legacies of antiquity itself. Almost inevitably given his educational and
social conditioning, he was an attentive reader of the minor as well as the
great Greek and Roman historians—Appian, Dio Cassius, Sallust and
Dionysius of Halicarnassus as well as Thucydides, Xenophon, Polybius,
Livy, Plutarch and Tacitus. From such sources he predictably culled
almost all of the material on ancient history which litters the pages of the
History in particular. From these same authorities also came the majority

of the evidence that Ferguson used to sustain his own arguments in the *Essay* and the *Principles*. But alongside the historians of Rome, he was also blessed with a profound knowledge of the ancient political theorists. Chief among these was, of course, Cicero, whose influence on Ferguson's social thought and moral philosophy we have already examined. Perhaps more important still, however, for Ferguson's political philosophy, was Aristotle himself, author of the *Politics*, which, albeit the fragmentary remains of a mutilated larger work, was still universally recognised in the eighteenth century as the epitome of ancient wisdom on the ageless questions of government and citizenship.

There are several key points that Ferguson appears to have derived directly from his intimate knowledge of the *Politics* and which underpin all of his own subsequent conclusions about the subject. First, and by some distance the most significant, he accepted, as Aristotle had taught, that man is by nature *zoon politikon*—which is to say, a political animal, in the sense that membership of a politically-organised community and, above all, an inclination to act in a public capacity, is a fundamental expression of a man's nature. Indeed, this proposition was so pregnant with implications that it provided at least some of Aristotle's successors with the basis of a much more far-reaching political theory in which direct participation in the business of government by all citizens (the latter category actually defined quite restrictively and usually limited to adult, male, property-owning non-slaves) amounted not merely to a desirable practical arrangement but even to the literal fulfillment of man's purpose as an essentially social creature. But Aristotle's seminal analysis, which ultimately came down strongly in favour of rule by the wise and the good rather than by the many, was also helpful in providing later writers with an understanding of how actual politics worked as well as with some commonplace assumptions about what the strengths and weaknesses of each distinct form of political organisation might characteristically be.

In fact, Aristotle's careful taxonomy of known political systems, or, more correctly, of existing states' constitutions, was to be immensely influential among subsequent theorists, and Ferguson was no exception. It was primarily this which would encourage Ferguson, as it had most recently encouraged Montesquieu in *The Spirit of the Laws* and Hume in his elegant political essays, to think that, at least in principle, governments could be divided into just three well-known types: monarchy, aristocracy and democracy. In Aristotle's view the rule of a wise and

benevolent monarch was the ideal form, followed in strict order of preference by an aristocratic regime under the benign control of men of
virtue and intelligence. But in practice, amid the unpromising conditions in the Greek world of his own day, he had been willing to accept
that a limited democracy was probably the best solution to the problem
of political organisation. Such judgments, and the standard typological framework for thinking about governments that he had definitively
established, were, as we shall see, Aristotle's principal bequests to the
Enlightenment in general and to Ferguson in particular.

Whilst Aristotle thus exerted a certain measure of direct control over
the formation of Ferguson's political philosophy, he was arguably to be of
even greater importance as an indirect influence. For, mediated through
a coherent body of political theory which had also passed through republican Rome, Renaissance Italy and Puritan England before finally alighting in eighteenth-century Scotland, Aristotle's conceptualisation of man
as *zoon politikon* was to have profound consequences for Ferguson's theory of citizenship. Indeed, both Ferguson's contemporaries and his later
readers have recognised that his ideas about man's place in political society belong squarely within this particular tradition of classically-based
theory, which is sometimes called 'classical republican' thought (in reference to its idealisation of the Athenian and Roman republics), but elsewhere (and rather more problematically) is described as 'Machiavellian'
or 'civic humanist'. Moreover, in this distinctive vision, it was always the
vita activa, the active life of which Cicero and certain other Stoics had
spoken so favourably, that was seen as being most in accord with man's
nature and consequently most likely to make him happy. It was also
through active participation in the public life of his community, including those core organisational activities—which we have learned to think
of as 'politics'—such as its formal supervision and physical protection,
that this ideal was most likely to be acted out.

Once these apparently straightforward philosophical premises were
accepted, however, theorists working within the republican tradition
were invariably convinced that some striking further conclusions must
follow. First, it was actually part of the very function of political society
to call forth and exercise those natural participatory instincts which alone
can make a man happy: as Machiavelli had insisted (and here it is very
much the strenuously republican Machiavelli of the *Discourses* (1519)
rather than the courtly sycophant behind *The Prince* (1513) that we have
in view), it was the privilege as much as the duty of citizens in a free state

to take an active part in the affairs of the community of which they were members. Second, it was accepted that all developments or impositions which tend in any way to limit or to jeopardise the citizens' direct participation in public life are necessarily retrograde. This latter argument inevitably led later theorists, as it would eventually lead Ferguson, to express notably caustic sentiments about those events during the final phase of the Roman republic, such as the turmoil introduced by the Gracchi and the careers of Marius and Sulla, which, at least in retrospect, appeared conspicuous milestones along the well-worn road to civil war and political catastrophe. But the same argument also had potentially awkward implications when applied to the analysis of modern European politics. For two of the most eye-catching trends in the organisation of advanced societies since the fifteenth century—namely the emergence of a distinct group of professional politicians and bureaucrats to manage the state's affairs and the creation of a class of professional (often mercenary) soldiers to fight its battles—clearly ran directly counter to the fundamental participatory principles of classical republican citizenship.

A third aspect of republican political theory by which Ferguson in particular was strongly touched was its habitual emphasis upon the very real possibility of a state entering into a process of relative or even terminal decline. In one sense this was merely a matter of facing facts. No previous writer in this tradition could have been unaware that to recount the virtues of republican societies or to sing the praises of the active citizen was also to rehearse a melancholy overture to a familiar and largely depressing opera—the defeat and death of the Athenian democracy; or the final destruction of the Roman republic by the usurper Octavian and his repellent imperial successors; or even, perhaps, the overthrow of the painfully short-lived Florentine republic by the Medici oligarchs (a revolution of which Machiavelli himself had been amongst the more prominent victims). But even aside from the bitter disappointments for republicanism that bespattered an exceptionally discouraging historical record, the theory of participatory citizenship also contained within it sufficient reason for real anxiety. For even its most ambitious proponents had had to accept that the fundamental causes of political decline— which, as they were by Ferguson too, were often placed under the catch-all heading of 'corruption'—were actually intrinsic and endemic in human society. In other words, the republican ideal was perpetually in peril from hostile forces which even unusual levels of citizenly virtue operating within a laudably well-wrought constitution would never entirely be able to suppress.

In particular, wealth was held to be a continual threat to the ethos of republics: merely the prospect, let alone the enjoyment, of personal enrichment, was believed to deflect citizens from their public duty and set selfishness and private jealousies loose within a previously united community. As a result, republican writers, in a strain of argument for which they were again able to borrow heavily from the other-worldly writings of several of the Stoic philosophers, were almost always viscerally hostile towards all manifestations of materialism. Certainly they tended to direct special scorn at those more extreme forms of consumption which they ritually denounced as 'luxury'—usually amounting to such heinous sins as the gratuitous accumulation of personal wealth or anything remotely smacking of ostentatious display. Similarly, political factionalism was an ever-present danger. This was especially so in republican societies which, according to their admirers, were meant to derive particular advantages from their exceptionally strong and cohesive sense of public spirit: by effectively driving wedges between citizen and citizen, and even perhaps tempting external enemies to strike opportunistically against a distracted and divided community, the tendency to form mutually-antagonistic parties, let alone to tolerate the spectacle of rival cliques of careerist politicians vying for exclusive control of the state's affairs, presented another obvious problem for those theorists who grounded their analysis particularly in the ultimately unhappy experiences of the Roman republic.

These inter-connected problems, and a series of hypothetical solutions to them, accordingly provided much of the focus in the more recent political writings from which Ferguson drew particular inspiration. From Machiavelli's *Discourses*, above all, he learned to look upon the fall of the Roman republic as a consequence of the loss of public spirit and the triumph of factionalism. From James Harrington, the English author of *The Commonwealth of Oceana* (1656), a visionary sketch of a free society governed in a participatory fashion by abstemious, patriotic property-owners, he acquired insights into how the enduring lessons of Roman politics might be reformulated so as to provide the basis of a powerful analysis of government and citizenship in the modern English-speaking world. Even more pertinently, Ferguson was intimately acquainted with the republican-infused writings of his colourful countryman, Andrew Fletcher of Saltoun. A leading Edinburgh parliamentarian and classical scholar at the turn of the eighteenth century, famous then and now as Scotland's most fervent opponent of the Treaty of Union, Fletcher may actually have been almost as familiar to Ferguson as the deceased uncle of his own powerful patron and sometime employer Lord Milton (indeed, beneath the noble courtesy title of a senior Scottish judge, the nephew actually shared the same name). But the elder Fletcher's writings—burning, said Ferguson's lawyer friend Sir John Dalrymple, with 'all the fire of ancient eloquence'—will have made anything but comfortable reading for a budding Enlightenment moral philosopher and social theorist who wished to unlock the secrets of political affairs (MGB I:6).

Fletcher, yet another passionate enthusiast for the virtues of republican Rome and for the 'excellent Rules of Government which the Antients have left us', had railed at prodigious length against a whole litany of contemporary ills which seemed to him to threaten an end to political liberties—at least as these had come to be understood by classically-obsessed, politically-active and intensely patriotic Scottish country gentlemen such as himself (DCM 4). Fletcher fretted over the eclipse of fixed landed property as the reliable foundation of national well-being and its replacement by an unfamiliar economic system increasingly dependent upon moveable commodities and rootless merchant networks. He was deeply suspicious about the proliferation of banking and credit facilities by the end of the seventeenth century, believing that they merely encouraged self-indulgent private consumption ('luxury', in Fletcher's terse demonology) and the dangerous bloating of the state's resources, even as they also inveigled the public into potentially ruinous debts. He greatly regreted the increase in the reach and authority of royal power, to the extent that he argued that government, in the hands of ambitious monarchs like William III and Louis XIV, was now largely impervious to the interests and opinions of most of its subjects. And in another move obviously aligning him with the distinctive concerns of earlier republican theorists, he also denounced the creation of permanent professional armies in states such as England and France. Indeed, Fletcher claimed that, because they lacked the natural ardour and selfless patriotism of the volunteer citizen militias whose rightful role they had usurped, these 'standing armies', whilst, of course, insufficiently motivated to provide effective protection against external enemies, were actually a useful tool in the untrustworthy hands of over-mighty rulers wishing to cow their own subjects into submission: no arrangement had ever been 'so essential to the Liberties of the People', he complained,

'as that which placed the Sword in the hands of the Subject' (DCM 6).
All of these familiar bogeys, cleverly identified by Fletcher with specific
events or trends in recent history, allowed him to launch an extraordinarily thought-provoking republican critique of modernity—and to that
extent of progress in some of its most characteristic forms—with which
the thinkers of the Scottish Enlightenment, themselves intrigued by the
contradictory implications of progress, clearly needed to grapple.

ii

Because of the considerable impact upon his writings of this extraordinarily rich intellectual heritage, it is easy enough to assign Ferguson's
theory of citizenship an exact position within that distinctive tradition of
political thought which begins with Aristotle and comes to rest, or rather
is given renewed vigour and potency, in eighteenth-century Scotland,
in the ceaselessly active person of Andrew Fletcher. Indeed, no propo-
nent of republican political thought in more than two thousand years
had more nearly embodied its central tenets than the singular laird of
Saltoun—a man still notorious two generations later, among the writers
of the Scottish Enlightenment, for the unlimited energy with which he
advanced his political views: 'his principles were thoroughly republican',
wrote one awe-struck historian in the 1770s, 'and he possessed con-
summate abilities, undaunted courage, and inflexible integrity' (NHS
272). The *vita activa*, so characteristic of Fletcher's political career as of
his political thought, was in turn to re-emerge as the main underlying
theme of Ferguson's own theory of citizenship. As he observes in an early
part of the *Essay*, whilst, significantly, attempting to instruct his readers
on that most Aristotelian of subjects, 'Of Happiness', which, as we saw
in Chapter 2, was understood as a fundamental objective that we are
destined to seek:

Happiness is not that state of repose, or that imaginary freedom from care, which
at a distance is so frequent an object of desire, but with its approach brings a
tedium, a languour, more unsupportable than pain itself. If the preceding observations on this subject be just, it arises more from the pursuit, than from the
attainment of any end whatever; and in every new situation to which we arrive,
even in the course of a prosperous life, it depends more on the degree in which
our minds are properly employed, than it does on the circumstances in which we
are destined to act, on the materials which are placed in our hands, or the tools
with which we are furnished. (E 51)

In short, precisely because of the construction of our natures, true human satisfaction and fulfillment is achieved not through rest but through activity—indeed, actually by the very process of *being* active, and being consciously engaged in an active pursuit, rather than simply by the desirable fruits that our labours may or may not eventually allow us to enjoy. 'All we can determine in general', says Ferguson, summarising in a later passage in the *Essay* this striking vision of man's supreme fittedness for active endeavour, 'is that whatever be the subjects with which he is engaged, the frame of his nature requires him to be occupied, and his happiness requires him to be just' (E 200).

As the concluding phrase in this last quotation hints, however, Ferguson also followed classical convention in linking the happiness attainable through the *vita activa* directly with life in a coherent community of other people. For it is not isolated, unseen or purely self-regarding acts which bring real satisfaction. Rather it is those forms of action which appear in full view of one's fellows. In a brilliant astronomical metaphor which illuminates another perceptibly republican-sounding section in Part V of the *Essay*, with the title 'Of the Temporary Effects and Relaxations of the National Spirit', Ferguson emphasises that it is in fact the public context to our actions which ultimately allows us most fully to assuage the urgent promptings of our nature:

If his errors and his crimes are the movements of an active being, his virtues and his happiness consist likewise in the employment of his mind; and all the lustre which he casts around him, to captivate or engage the attention of his fellow-creatures, like the flame of a meteor, shines only when his motion continues: the moments of rest and of obscurity are the same. (E 199)

Ferguson also insists upon the related point, again particularly well-explained in the *Essay* in the section 'Of Happiness', that it is actually public spiritedness and a proper sense of duty to the community that provides a man with the noblest expression of the *vita activa*:

The members of those illustrious states, from the habit of considering themselves part of a community, or at least as deeply involved with some order of men in the state, were regardless of personal considerations: they had a perpetual view to objects which excite a great ardour in the soul; which led them to act perpetually in the view of their fellow-citizens, and to practise those arts of deliberation, elocution, policy, and war, on which the fortunes of nations, or of men, in their collective body, depend. (E 57)

The principle on which Fergsuon's political philosophy is founded, then, is that it is indeed the public, and not the personal, that should be the over-riding consideration in our actions. It is this alone that will bring us the true happiness which it is in our nature to desire.

We should note, however, that Ferguson alleges here that this remarkable state of affairs had nevertheless been the norm in what he calls 'those illustrious states': as he elaborates a few lines later, lest anyone be unclear as to the point that he has in mind, 'To the ancient Greek, or the Roman, the individual was nothing, and the public every thing. To the modern, in too many nations of Europe, the individual is every thing, and the public nothing'. In other words, a life of vigorous activity oriented towards one's community was seen by Ferguson as the highest expression of a man's nature. But, as the reference to specific historical precedents also makes clear, this was no mere hypothetical principle, without serious practical applications. In fact, Ferguson's interest in the possibility of eighteenth-century people actually being able to emulate the active and public-spirited citizens of antiquity may help explain his reaction to the French Revolution, towards which, as we have seen, he was, at least in private, markedly less hostile than many of his Scottish contemporaries. After all, despite the imminent military threat that it posed to Britain, revolutionary France, which encouraged direct participation in public affairs by a significant portion of the citizenry, seemed to represent a unique—and, to judge from the revolutionaries' rhetoric, a self-conscious—experiment in the modern revival of the classical republican ideal. For this reason if for no other, the Revolution was always likely to arouse at least some intellectual curiosity and sneaking sympathy in a man with Ferguson's essentially Roman preferences in politics.

It was with this fundamental aspect to man's existence securely established in his political philosophy that Ferguson was able to build an extensive theory of citizenship upon the firmest of classical foundations. The section 'Of Civil Liberty' in Part III of the *Essay* is probably the most important exposition of this argument, beginning with its studied re-emphasis upon the embodiment of the *vita activa* in a life of specifically public-oriented endeavour: 'It is in conducting the affairs of civil society', Ferguson writes at one point, 'that mankind find the exercise of their best talents, as well as the object of their best affections' (E 149). One consequence of this philosophical commitment to the *vita activa*, which was sometimes found elsewhere in Ferguson's Scottish circle, was that it made it much easier to explain why certain states, and particularly the ancient republics, had been so successful. Even Robertson, normally less inclined to republicanism than Ferguson, had felt able to tell the readers of his *History of Scotland* that it was in the small states of antiquity that all of man's finer impulses had been freely displayed—'temperance, frugality, decency, public-spirit, love to their fellow citizens, magnanimity'—and that accordingly 'on this foundation of public liberty did ancient virtue rest' (HS 15). As Ferguson puts the same point in a slightly different way in the *Principles*:

The history of mankind has confirmed our conjecture in this matter: It has abundantly shewn, in the instance of republican governments, that the attainments of knowledge, ability, and public virtue, are proportioned to the concern which numbers are permitted to take, in the affairs of their community; and to the exertion of ingenuity and public spirit, which they have occasion to make in national counsels, in offices of state, or public services of any sort. (P I:266)

In the *Essay*, meanwhile, in a manoeuvre which speaks volumes about the emphatically republican lineage in which Ferguson's political thinking so obviously stands, he was able to develop an analysis not so much of the operations and merits of active citizenship as of the familiar obstacles standing in its way.

Sparta was particularly useful for this purpose. Famed equally for its ferocious military capabilities and for its stolid insistence upon minimising material inequality between its citizens, that state had relentlessly pursued a form of pure republicanism from which even Athens and Rome had fallen significantly short. In fact, Sparta's sumptuary laws, seeking to exert a measure of public control over personal consumption and property ownership, were of special fascination precisely because they had clearly been a singular attempt, as a fascinated Ferguson described it, 'to shut up this source of corruption', namely 'the gratification of vanity', 'the ostentation of superior fortune' and 'the desire of riches' (E 152). Quoting approvingly from Xenophon, it was therefore evident to Ferguson that there was one reason above all why, in the Greek world, 'the Spartans should excel every nation': it was because they had also been 'the only state in which virtue is studied as the object of government' (E 153).

Yet Ferguson's interest in classical republicanism, as his ambivalent attitudes towards the French Revolution should remind us, was in no sense reducible to the empty veneration of arcane and antiquated precedents. Indeed, one living expression of the participatory principle that

was still very much prospering in the eighteenth century—namely, a
respect for the rule of law because a state's laws are perceived by those
under its jurisdiction to be fairly and consistently applied—was in
Ferguson's view another of the practical cornerstones of a successful,
stable and essentially virtuous polity. Here, too, however, Ferguson felt
it necessary to offer his readers some interesting judgments about the
particular historical conditions in which this crucial political ideal might
actually be attained:

> Rome and England, under their mixed governments, the one inclining to democ-
> racy, the other to monarchy, have proved the great legislators among nations...
> Under such favourable establishments, known customs, the practice and deci-
> sions of courts, as well as positive statutes, acquire the authority of laws; and
> every proceeding is conducted by some fixed and determinate rule. (E 159)

Ancient precedent, in other words, was clearly capable of the most direct
of contemporary applications. But Ferguson had also noticed something
else very important about the peculiar way in which both republican
Rome in antiquity and England in the present day had apparently
organised their legal systems:

> . . . a surprising coincidence is found in the singular methods of their jurisdic-
> tion. The people in both reserved in a manner the office of judgement to them-
> selves, and brought the decision of civil rights, or of criminal questions, to the
> tribunal of peers, who, in judging of their fellow-citizens, prescribed a condition
> of life for themselves. (E 159–60)

On this reading, participation had been the distinguishing feature of
the most successful and long-lasting states throughout civilised history.
In England as in Rome, the citizens were personally implicated in the
creation and administration of the law. Active public involvement of this
sort, according to Ferguson, even explained the unusual degree of authority and legitimacy that these structures plainly enjoyed: it conferred a
genuine sense of common ownership of the state, and, as a result, an
almost religious zeal among its citizens for its care and service that boded
especially well for its defence and future prosperity. As Ferguson reiter-
ates this important claim in the *History*, with an approving allusion to
a similar argument in Machiavelli's *Discourses* which had linked citizen
participation first to patriotism and then on to political strength, 'the
seeds of Roman greatness were laid in the implicit respect with which
every citizen revered the first institutions of his country' (H 12).

Active citizenship was also closely linked with another major facet of Ferguson's analysis, that which concerned itself with military affairs—a subject to which, like all earlier republican theorists, he turned, as we have seen, with undisguised relish. Ferguson's *Essay* certainly could have left his contemporaries in little doubt that the development of standing armies, comprising not a cohort of public-spirited members of the community but a select body of primarily financially-motivated hirelings, brought all manner of disadvantages in its wake. In reflections presented to his readers under what to any self-satisfied Hanoverian Briton in the later 1760s must have been a somewhat unnerving title, 'Of Relaxations in the National Spirit incident to Polished Nations', Ferguson even offers the model republican critique—*pace* Andrew Fletcher—of the disastrous military consequences of the kind of occupational specialisation which had latterly turned the public themselves into strangers to the arts of war:

If the defence and government of a people be made to depend on a few, who make the conduct of state or of war their profession; whether these be foreigners or natives; whether they be called away of a sudden, like the Roman legion from Britain; whether they turn against their employers, like the army of Carthage, or be over-powered and dispersed by a stroke of fortune, the multitude of cowardly and undisciplined people must, on such an emergence, receive a foreign or a domestic enemy, as they would a plague or an earthquake, with hopeless amazement and terror... (E 215–6)

Such were inevitably the main lessons about a state's international standing that were to be drawn from the Roman experience in particular. But, as Ferguson lamented in the *Essay*, there were also likely to be catastrophic domestic implications too. For the emergence of self-obsessed careerist generals and of rapacious mercenary armies under their command had also soon spelled the end of republican liberties at home:

The Romans only meant by their armies to incroach on the freedoms of other nations, while they preserved their own. They forgot, that in assembling soldiers of fortune, and in suffering any leader to be master of a disciplined army, they actually resigned their political rights, and suffered a master to arise for the state. (E 219)

The fate of the Roman republic, then, proved beyond doubt that the citizens' jealously-guarded right to participate actively in public endeavours was itself a necessary, if not a sufficient, condition for the survival of liberty, and even for the continued existence of the state itself. And it was this principle above all which had been breached—in recent times as well as in antiquity—by the emergence of armies that were both permanent in duration and mercenary in character.

That Ferguson's evident distaste for standing armies, mostly on political grounds, was far from unique in mid-eighteenth-century Britain, is also worth strongly underlining. For this characteristic trope of the classical republican tradition, ultimately rooted in Aristotle's emphasis upon the *vita activa* but increasingly tied since the Renaissance to the specific problems posed by armies and military organisation, influenced many of Scotland's other leading social theorists: even John Millar, for example, who perhaps least fits the stereotype of the republican ideologue, felt it necessary to assert that a standing army in the hands of a monarch—as Fletcher himself might have put it—amounted to 'the great engine of tyranny and oppression' (ODR 188). Nor are the peculiar topical attractions of this kind of analysis to Scottish philosophers between the mid-1760s and the late 1780s all that difficult to identify. Indeed, given Britain's own increasingly parlous position, with the shattering loss of the American colonies, with the nation's professional military machine apparently outfoxed by the French and the Spanish, and with a fatal combination of luxury and corruption widely believed to be overwhelming the constitution at home, these eternal lessons about the sustaining link between virtue, virility and military vigour had, at least in the eyes of many of Ferguson's contemporaries, never been more germane. Small wonder, then, that the Scottish financier and City banker Thomas Coutts, writing in 1783 to his friend Colonel Crawfurd, should have claimed to see in the pages of Ferguson's newly-published *History*, which relayed this same alarming message at even greater length than had the earlier *Essay*, 'what our country is fast coming to. Rome was never more venal that we are already' (C I:lxvii).

iii

Ferguson, the former Black Watch officer and tireless (if long-frustrated) campaigner for Scotland's right to form a volunteer militia, was plainly intrigued as a political philosopher by the role of military service in the life of the individual citizen and, potentially, of course, in the final implosion of a state. But closely related to this preoccupation with military organisation was the prominence which his political theory accorded to the causes and character of conflict as it flared periodically not only within but also between societies. For in an obvious sense the preponderance of warfare in man's existence was merely another logical deduction from the commonplace belief that a man's purpose in life was to pursue unceasingly the *vita activa*. Indeed, on this interpretation conflict could be understood simply as an extreme form of human dynamism. It was the ultimate expression of man's intrinsic passion for political engagement, and, in practical terms, an effective means to the attainment of his perfectly natural inclination for ownership, power and status: 'where the fermentation is most violent, the purest spirits are sometimes extracted', as this was put metaphorically by John Gillies, one of Smith's Glasgow students and, as one of Britain's leading Greek historians, eventually Robertson's successor as Historiographer-Royal for Scotland (OLI civ). At the same time, when placed in the context of relations between states, to borrow Clausewitz's later dictum, warfare really was capable of being understood simply as 'the continuation of political intercourse, carried on with other means' (OW 87). Yet the link back to Ferguson's theory of citizenship, and what seems at times almost an obsession with the need in the life of the truly virtuous and happy individual for continual public involvement, also explains much about his interest in the social and psychological implications of conflict.

It should not therefore be surprising that Ferguson explicitly describes conflict to his readers as both an inevitable and a normal consequence of man's social instincts. Indeed, he seems to have considered that it would be extremely difficult even to conceive of a community—that other natural product of man's innate sociability—which harboured no appetite at all for violent competition with its rivals. As Ferguson explained in the key early section in Part I of the *Essay* entitled 'Of the principles of War and Dissension' (tellingly, Ferguson placed it directly following the section 'Of the principles of Union among Mankind', almost as though it were simply the other side of the same coin): 'Without the rivalship of nations, and the practice of war, civil society itself could scarcely have found an object, or a form' (E 28). Moreover, this disposition to rivalry and disagreement between men has its roots in the frame of our natures:

Mankind not only find in their condition the sources of variance and dissension; they appear to have in their minds the seeds of animosity, and to embrace the occasions of mutual opposition, with alacrity and pleasure. In the most pacific situation there are few who have not their enemies, as well as their friends; and who are not pleased with opposing the proceedings of one, as much as with favouring the designs of another. (E 25)

In other words, conflict is not merely very common in our experience. It is also effectively unavoidable, because it is, at bottom, just one more instinctive and irrepressible expression of our natural proclivities.

Yet, rather more controversially, Ferguson also believed that individual men benefit from participation in that conflict towards which nature itself has pointed them. This is because their powers and capabilities are actually never more clearly expressed and exhibited, nowhere more likely to be honed and improved, than in those intensely competitive human activities of which military combat is in many respects the purest, most demanding, and most revealing form. Ferguson, perhaps again speaking as a former regimental chaplain with first-hand experience of European battlefields, was even prepared to claim that a man who had never felt, or who was for some other reason unable to share, the powerful passions aroused by conflict, was, in an absolutely critical sense, stripped of an essential element of his own humanity. As the *Essay* asserts:

To overawe, or intimidate, or, when we cannot persuade with reason, to resist with fortitude, are the occupations which give its most animating exercise, and its greatest triumphs, to a vigorous mind; and he who has never struggled with his fellow-creatures, is a stranger to half the sentiments of mankind. (E 28)

These opinions are also buttressed once more by reference to a host of historical examples, all of which suggest the universality of this psychological pattern and, consequently, the prevalence of conflict and competition between men. As a result, Ferguson is able to ask, in another piece of the elevated rhetoric in which the *Essay* abounds:

What is it that stirs in the breasts of ordinary men when the enemies of their country are named? Whence are the prejudices that subsist between different provinces, cantons, and villages, of the same empire and territory? What is it that excites one half of the nations of Europe against the other? (E 27)

The answer to each question, of course, is that these sentiments originate in the deepest recesses of our own minds. Certainly, thinks Ferguson, they are not foisted upon otherwise peace-loving men by the unscrupulous devices of self-serving and ambitious leaders—as those who imagine warfare to be unnatural and aberrant have often insinuated. Rather they are an elemental expression of people's very natures, to which, indeed, high-minded legislators and squeamish politicians alike have frequently responded with genuine horror and alarm: 'it is among them that we find the materials for war and dissension laid without the direction of government, and sparks ready to kindle into flame', says Ferguson emphatically, 'which the statesman is frequently disposed to extinguish' (E 27).

It follows for Ferguson that civil society too is a beneficiary of the experience of conflict. This is particularly true in the sense that warfare, in arousing strongly patriotic sentiments, and in the necessity it creates for individual men to commit themselves clearly and decisively to their comrades' and the wider public's interests, tends ordinarily to enhance the sympathetic ties which naturally bind a community together: 'Patriotism is enflamed by a struggle for liberty, by a civil war', as Kames too observed (SHM I:441). In the *Essay*, in a passage which invites parallels with Ferguson's continuing campaign for a Scottish militia after the 1750s, as well as with his sense during the 1790s that revolutionary France positively wished for the continuation of the European wars, this point is made very clearly:

The sense of a common danger, and the assaults of an enemy, have been frequently useful to nations, by uniting their members more firmly together, and by preventing the secessions and actual separations in which their civil discord might otherwise terminate. (E 26)

But this important principle has still wider—and even more controversial—implications than might at first appear. For this social benefit will apparently accrue whether the warfare in question is defensive or aggressive, just or unjust. As he admits, 'The frequent practice of war tends to strengthen the bands of society, and the practice of depredation itself engages men in trials of mutual attachment and courage' (E 99). This is surely the philosophical assumption that also lies behind Ferguson's extraordinarily daring proposal for dealing with the French threat in the 1790s, in which he argued for containment rather than confrontation. As Ferguson explains in a surviving letter of 1796 to Sir John Macpherson, simply removing any opportunities for the French to wage war would deny what was effectively a republic of active citizens the main source of its new-found strength: indeed, continuing to subject such a state to external threats, and thereby giving it the chance to redouble its military and political energies, was in Ferguson's judgment merely like 'probing the wild beasts to make him foam & Roar' (C II:397).

At the same time, the seemingly limitless scope for the generation of corruption, that all-purpose solvent of the cohesion and integrity of established political communities, was particularly feared by Ferguson where it had essentially military origins. For it was a necessary consequence of the individual and communal benefits of the experience of warfare that those innovations which tended to remove the opportunity for citizens to participate actively in conflict brought with them potentially disastrous implications. This was, of course, a further point of contact for Ferguson with the anxieties about standing armies with which the classical republican tradition had always been shot through. But it was also an argument which linked directly with his immediate political concerns in mid-eighteenth-century Scotland about the consequences of the country not being permitted to form its own militia. As Ferguson notes in the section of the *Essay* titled 'Of National Defense and Conquest':

In the progress of arts and of policy, the members of every state are divided into classes; and in the commencement of this distribution, there is no distinction more serious than that of the warrior and the pacific inhabitants; no more is required to place men in the relation of master and slave. (E 145)

With this unwelcome and specifically political implication of military specialisation acknowledged, Ferguson also required his readers to consider, as he puts it, 'the breach that such an establishment makes in the system of national virtues', as well as the fact that 'it is unpleasant to observe, that most nations who have run the career of civil arts, have, in some degree, adopted this measure' (E 146). In other words, the development of standing armies and professional soldiers, as Hanoverian Britain was now demonstrating only too completely for Ferguson's comfort, were an apparently normal concomitant of the degree of advancement attained by modern society. But, whatever the other benefits brought by specialisation—with which in purely economic contexts, as we have seen, Ferguson had little complaint—when applied also to the military sphere it threatened simultaneously the precious virtues of the citizen and the moral fabric of the political community.

iv

Ferguson's emphasis upon the constant participation of active (almost, it appears, hyper-active) citizens in the life of the community was, as we have seen, an aspect of his political philosophy which clearly looked directly back to the decidedly mixed fortunes of the ancient republics, as well as having striking resonances in his own experiences, unusual in an Enlightenment philosopher, as a younger man in the British army. His fascination with conflict, given the extraordinary triumphs which those republics—and Rome above all—had commonly enjoyed, obviously had roots in essentially the same hallowed soil. Less specifically Roman, though still something of which close scrutiny of the successive Roman constitutions would necessarily have formed an integral part, was Ferguson's keen interest in the various forms of political organisation that a community might in principle decide to adopt. Indeed, in this respect his theory of government bears comparison with those of many previous commentators. But this was no mere academic exercise in the scholarly criticism of earlier work in a densely-crowded field. Rather, Ferguson was concerned to establish quite precisely the merits and defects of different kinds of constitution for two essentially practical purposes. The first was his need for a philosophical account of government consistent with his own theory of citizenship: Ferguson, after all, thought that goverments should be judged according to whether or not they were conducive to the freedom and fulfillment—or, to use the terms that he would have preferred, the activity and so the ultimate happiness—of the citizen. The second purpose was to allow him to probe the credentials of a number of the contemporary regimes with which his eighteenth-century students and readers would be immediately familiar.

In relation to the relative merits of the three distinct types of government on which authorities such as Aristotle, Polybius, Cicero and Montesquieu had all written, the most striking feature of Ferguson's analysis to the modern reader is likely to be its almost sociological flavour. For Ferguson is adamant that, like all other social constructions, an individual system of government is simply the product of one specific set of historical circumstances: as a result, whilst almost by definition appropriate to its original context, it is equally likely to be inappropriate in another. As he explains in 'Of National Felicity', in a key passage of the *Essay* towards the close of Part I, section 9:

Forms of government are supposed to decide of the happiness or misery of mankind. But forms of government must be varied, in order to suit the extent, the way of subsistence, the character, and the manners of different nations. In some cases the multitude may be suffered to govern themselves; in others, they must be severely restrained. The inhabitants of a village in some primitive age, may have been safely intrusted to the conduct of reason, and to the suggestion of their innocent views; but the tenants of Newgate can scarcely be trusted, with chains locked to their bodies, and bars of iron fixed to their legs. How is it possible, therefore, to find any single form of government that would suit mankind in every condition? (E 63)

This explicit political relativism, based on an understanding of the context-specific modes of human behaviour and social culture upon which any viable system of political organisation must ultimately rest, is what underlies Ferguson's analysis of the various forms of constitution which history, and the traditional canons of classical theory, had bequeathed to him.

The far-reaching implications of this quasi-sociological assumption become evident as Ferguson attempts to identify the respective qualities of monarchy, aristocracy and democracy, particularly as these are itemised in the succeeding section of the *Essay*. In the first instance, it enables him to establish the historical context to which each type of constitution is, he believes, especially suited. Ferguson claims, for example, that monarchies 'are generally found, where the state is enlarged in population and in territory, beyond the numbers and dimensions that are consistent with republican government' (E 69). At the same time, opportunities for active political participation are still very much a part of monarchy in Ferguson's view: as he also says, 'the subjects of monarchies, like those of republics, find themselves occupied as the members of an active society, and engaged to treat with their fellow-creatures on a liberal footing' (E 71). Indeed, it appears to be the case in monarchies that 'every individual, in his separate capacity, in some measure, deliberates for his country' (E 70–1). Of course, Ferguson does not mean 'every individual' in a literal sense: rather he has in mind the responsible and far-sighted propertied male citizenry, since, as he would specifically point out in rejecting what he considered the extreme demands of the American revolutionaries, 'the essence of political Liberty is such an establishment as gives power to the wise, and safety to all' (RPEM 9). Even so, as Montesquieu had also argued, monarchy, instead of exhibiting this attractively republican capacity for enlisting the energies of the respectable and patriotic citizen, was also capable of being horribly corrupted, and of mutating into a distinctly less appealing system, that form of personal rule known technically as 'despotism'. In these circumstances, by contrast with true monarchy, as Ferguson says in the *Essay*, 'the subject is told, that he has no rights; that he cannot possess any property, nor fill any station, independent of the momentary will of his prince': despotism is, in short, an essentially deviant form of monarchical government in which opportunities for public activity by the populace, as well as other key political rights, are effectively truncated (E 71).

Ferguson's substantially favourable analysis of monarchy, which he paints as a moderate and, most strikingly, comparatively participatory form of government, was clearly strongly influenced by his own personal commitment to the wealthy, sophisticated, stable and relatively free society of Hanoverian Britain. It is also not difficult to see why Ferguson is at pains to avoid the classical tendency to identify monarchy straightforwardly with despotism: like Montesquieu, he thinks this equation misconceived, a reflection of the outdated prejudices of anti-autocratic theorists like Aristotle and Machiavelli rather than a sober and historically-sensitive evaluation of monarchy as it actually exists in eighteenth-century commercial societies. Indeed, this is doubtless why Ferguson adds in the *Essay*, immediately after his analysis of monarchy and clearly *apropos* the conventional constitutional taxonomy to which most earlier theorists had been tied, that 'Whilst we thus, with so much accuracy, can assign the ideal limits that may distinguish constitutions of government, we find them, in reality, both in respect to the principle and the form, variously blended together' (E 71). It is certainly also why in the *Institutes*, which, of course, distilled the essence of the political doctrines Ferguson presented to his Edinburgh student audiences, we find an alternative two-fold division of all constitutions merely into 'The simple, and the mixed', with the former comprising all three of the familiar Aristotelian categories and the latter, as Ferguson glosses it, 'a plurality of collateral powers' (I 42–3).

Ferguson's treatment of democracy—which is to say, of the participatory republican polity in its purest form—is similarly influenced by his deep personal loyalty to the existing Hanoverian constitution, some of whose most vociferous and dangerous critics increasingly espoused radically democratic principles. But it is also shaped by a keen awareness that, once again, he is better placed than earlier theorists to situate this particular form of government in its proper historical perspective. Above all, Ferguson considers that it is a fundamental problem with democracy that, as he again seems to have told his students, this form of government has clearly been most characteristic of 'states of small extent'— which is to say, like Athens and Rome, with populations and territories inconsequential by eighteenth-century standards (I 293). It also seems obvious to Ferguson that democracy, whose extremely participatory political culture necessarily functions best where there are only minor inequalities between the citizens, is better suited to the first rather than to the later stages of man's development, before the growth of wealth begins to create wide disparities in income. Furthermore, Ferguson is prepared to concede that slightly larger states—those of 'various extent', as he ambiguously describes them—might also be capable of maintaining a democratic system, providing that no substantial wealth, and so no great social inequality, has arisen. Yet he also insists that, where a complex economy and elaborate social hierarchy has indeed begun to emerge, the resulting society will instead establish a constitution better suited to its new circumstances—either 'aristocratical government, or... a mixed republic' (if it still remains relatively small in scale) or a 'mixed monarchy' (if the state has finally expanded to a much greater extent) (I 295–7). With this carefully constructed and highly tendentious analysis, Ferguson had effectively boxed-in participatory democracy in its most radical form, suggesting that on clear historical grounds it was—and, by deliberate implication, that it should always be—confined to contexts such as those known in ancient times to the classical Athenians and the early Romans.

Having dismissed the notion of full-blown participatory democracy as a system of political organisation unsuited to the modern era, the way obviously lay open for Ferguson in both his writings and his lectures to explore an even more significant result of his having conceded the possibility of substantial practical mixture between the different ideal forms of government. For it was this which created the opportunity for Ferguson to advance a coherent case for mixed monarchy, itself a recognisably composite form of constitution where, to quote the neat summary offered in the *Institutes*, 'the supreme power has been sometimes shared betwixt a king and nobles, or betwixt a king, nobles, and people' (I 45). Montesquieu had already asserted the superiority of a balanced or mixed constitution (which, as a committed anglophile, he readily took eighteenth-century England's to be) on the convenient grounds that it had the ability to combine the characteristic virtues, yet also to avoid the trademark vices, of each individual form of government. But from Ferguson's point of view, there were at least two other strong arguments to be heard in favour of mixed monarchy in modern times. First, and very much following the same procedure as he had adopted to present the development of other forms of government in relativist terms, he was able to insist that mixed monarchy was actually the form of government best suited to the size, social structure and economic conditions obtaining specifically in an advanced or 'polished' society: in other words, at the risk of blatant circularity, it was Ferguson's contention that government along the lines practiced in, for example, modern Britain, was desirable because it was a system which had emerged naturally to suit the peculiar conditions found in highly-developed commercial states—like, obviously, modern Britain. Ferguson's other argument in favour of mixed monarchy was, however, somewhat less relativist (and much less tautological): it amounted to the confident assertion that, of all the many different forms of constitution developed at any point in history, mixed monarchy was in fact the best suited to the essential purposes of government.

Ferguson's attempts to justify mixed monarchy by reference to the peculiar context created by an advanced society drew powerful inspiration from his broader social theory, as well as from his belief in some of the main principles of philosophical history. For in Ferguson's analysis, notably laid out in an intriguing section of the *Essay* entitled 'The History of Subordination', mixed monarchy appears as the largely unintentional outcome of a lengthy process of negotiation and arbitration through successive phases of social development between the competing demands of kings, noblemen and people. In some cases, of course, a very different answer to the problem of increasingly-complex social structures had been devised by ambitious kings. But their actions had really only 'paved the way for despotism in the state': as Ferguson describes this royal strategy of simply arrogating more and more power to the sovereign ruler as sole arbiter in society, 'with the same policy by which they relieved the subject from many oppressions, they increased the powers of the crown' (E 128). Of course, what Ferguson has in reality managed here is to provide an explanation for the emergence of the absolutist monarchs—'the princes of Europe', as he calls them—who between them ruled over the eighteenth-century Continent: France, Austria, Prussia, Spain and Russia.

The peculiar virtue of mixed monarchy, according to Ferguson, is that, by contrast, it achieves the same stability by accommodating the different aspirations of society's diverse constituencies and interest groups within the very structure of government. Nor is this all. As Ferguson explains the additional unique benefits to the readers of the *Essay*:

where the people had by the constitution a representative in the government, and a head, under which they could avail themselves of the wealth they acquired, and of the sense of their personal importance, this policy turned against the crown; it formed a new power to restrain the prerogative, to establish the government of law, and to exhibit a spectacle new in the history of mankind; monarchy mixed with republic, and extensive territory, governed, during some ages, without military force. (E 128)

Not only has mixed monarchy diverted such societies away from the road which otherwise might well have led to despotism. It has simultaneously provided perfectly for the peaceful government of a free society. Mixed monarchy is therefore evidently a superior solution to the increasing difficulties faced as society advances towards commerce and politeness. Indeed, it even incorporates many of the advantages classically ascribed to republics alone: for example, in incorporating a number of conflicting interest groups, it necessarily creates the potential for a modest degree of internal factional conflict. Yet providing that these constructive tensions do not reach levels sufficient to fracture the unity of the state, they can even be welcomed as a further opportunity for political activity among the citizens, and certainly will not pose the kind of threat that they had done to the republics of antiquity: as Ferguson puts this point in the *Institutes*, 'The spirit of faction that in republics constituted corruption, in monarchies tends to prevent a greater corruption, servility to those in power' (I 313). And again seeming to revive one of the best traits of the ancient republics, mixed monarchy actually appears to be notably protective of the rights and interests of the public at large: 'In governments properly mixed', Ferguson asserts in the *Essay*'s key section 'Of Civil Liberty', 'the popular interest, finding a counterpoise in that of the prince or of the nobles, a balance is actually established between them, in which the public freedom and the public order are made to consist' (E 158).

Mixed monarchy is thus the best system of political organisation for a 'polished' society in particular. But it is also, in Ferguson's view, the most desirable form of constitution among all those to which human history has yet given witness. The kernel of this more ambitious argument lies in Ferguson's opinion, as we have already seen, that a capacity for making viable and workable laws for the orderly regulation of society is the most significant practical function of any state: 'there is a necessity for law', he tells us in the *Essay*, 'and there are a variety of interests to be adjusted in framing every statute' (E 158). Ferguson also argues that Britain is once again a particularly good example of this process in action, with specific laws, widely accepted not only by the people but even by the king and nobility, showing how a balance can be struck which preserves the most precious of liberties:

> We must admire, as the key-stone of civil liberty, the statute which forces the secrets of every prison to be revealed, the cause of every commitment to be declared, and the person of the accused to be produced, that he may claim his enlargement, or his trial, within a limited time. No wiser form was ever opposed to the abuses of power. But it requires a fabric no less than the whole political constitution of Great Britain, a spirit no less than the refractory and turbulent zeal of this fortunate people, to secure its effects. (E 160)

With this bold conclusion, of course, we also arrive back, finally, at Ferguson's fundamental attachment to the *vita activa* and to participatory citizenship. Never better nurtured in modern times, he says, than by the 'refractory and turbulent zeal' of the British people, it is a deep-rooted tradition of active public involvement in the operation of a mixed monarchy, and the consequent respect and reverence which the rule of law enjoys among the populace, which are the truly remarkable features of Britain's present constitution. For here, Ferguson suggests, is a modern commercial society which has 'carried the authority and government of law to a point of perfection, which they never before attained in the history of mankind', yet which is also able to offer a space in which might still be acted out the classical political virtues on which the greatness of Rome itself was once founded (E 159).

v

Ferguson's political philosophy, as we have seen, was, first and foremost, informed by a profound reverence towards the city-states of the ancient Mediterranean world, and particularly towards republican Rome, which earlier theorists had also frequently shared: 'To know it well', he writes in the *History*, 'is to know mankind; and to have seen our species under the fairest aspect of great ability, integrity, and courage' (H 10). It was this model which suggested to him the pre-eminent value of participation in public life, itself the ultimate expression of the *vita activa* which allowed a man to approach—even, perhaps, occasionally to have the chance of attaining—the virtue and the happiness that were the proper object of his existence. Active citizenship, manifested in debate, in voting, in political engagement, in the administration of the law, and, in its purest and starkest expressions, experienced through military service and combat, was therefore central to Ferguson's thinking. Yet it was difficult—and increasingly so for an inhabitant of mid-eighteenth-century Europe's most commercially and militarily dynamic state—to reconcile this classically-derived ideal with the changing political realities which history had since revealed. Ultimately, this was why Ferguson was prepared to concede that the ancient republic itself, to inspirational predecessors like Machiavelli and Fletcher still the perfect vehicle for the pursuit of citizenly virtue, was neither a possible nor even a remotely appropriate model for the utterly different circumstances found in the large, wealthy and complex societies of Ferguson's own day.

Instead, but still on recognisably classical grounds, and essentially by the curious device of clothing it in quasi-republican form, Ferguson was able to present mixed monarchy as the best possible constitution for the conditions faced by modern Europeans—and even in some respects as the finest form of political organisation yet invented by man. But Ferguson's preoccupation with conflict, and his greater anxiety about the danger of corruption, simultaneously made him less optimistic about modern states, even those blessed with a mixed monarchy, than either Montesquieu or Hume. Indeed, Ferguson's republican preconceptions still led him to talk with surprising vehemence about the peculiar advantages supposedly brought to men and to their governments by the regular experience of warfare. These same concerns also brought him continually back to the threat to public virtue, and thus to the survival of states, posed by the worrying tendency towards political specialisation and military professionalism, both of which happened to be conspicuous features of all advanced societies. The result was an analysis in which idealism needed to be tempered by reality, the seductive symmetries of theory balanced against the practical lessons taught by modern history. Such fruitful tensions ensured that Ferguson's political philosophy was blissfully inconsistent—with its curious plea for a republican kind of monarchy, for an order and stability strangely facilitated by interminable contests and vigour, for a wealthy society of commercial professionals to be defended by an abstemious and austere legion of patriotic amateurs. As he had himself described this peculiar amalgam of concerns in a revealing phrase in his pamphlet on the militia issue in 1756, the aim was essentially 'to mix the military spirit with our civil and commercial policy' (RPEM 3). This was almost certainly what made Ferguson's political ideas so profoundly resonant in the circumstances of late-eighteenth-century Britain, where such choices, between republican principles and modernity, were still being faced. But it was also what made them, as we shall see in the next chapter, singularly difficult to translate into the very different conditions, emphatically modern in character, that were increasingly familiar to Ferguson's nineteenth-century readers.

Chapter Six

"I Had Almost Said Universal Success": Impact and Influence

In the nearly two-and-a-half centuries since Adam Ferguson's first and most innovative work was published, the history of attitudes towards his ideas and his achievements as a thinker has been exceptionally complex. There has, unfortunately, been no continuous acknowledgement of Ferguson as a theorist of the first rank—as there has been, for example, of his friends Smith in political economy and Hume in philosophy. But nor has there been a tendency simply for his reputation gradually and gracefully to fade—the fate which arguably has befallen some of his other Scottish colleagues, once celebrated but now largely forgotten, like Beattie the moralist and Blair the sermoniser and literary critic. Rather, Ferguson's literary and intellectual standing has suffered considerable alterations at the hands of successive generations, his great early fame giving way to an almost total obscurity, and then, finally, in recent decades, to a dramatic and quite unexpected recovery of reputation and stature. Indeed, these extraordinary fluctuations in Ferguson's presumed significance are frozen, for all to see, in the extremely odd publication history of the *Essay* itself.

Whilst seven English editions alone had appeared by the time of Ferguson's death in 1814, in addition to numerous foreign imprints and translations in locations as distant and diverse as Basle, Leipzig, Paris and Boston, no single further nineteenth-century edition was actually attempted anywhere after that time: indeed by 1876, Sir Leslie Stephen, whose writings represent late-Victorian literary scholarship at its most opinionated, could dismiss Ferguson without a second thought as merely 'a facile and dexterous declaimer' (HET II: 182). Yet, building upon the modest beginnings established by the two German editions of the *Essay* ventured in the first half of the twentieth century, a succession of separate English editions or re-prints, not to mention a continuing stream of French, German, Spanish, Chinese and Japanese translations, has been issued since 1966. Clearly, then, if we wish to understand why Ferguson's achievements have always provoked such strongly contrasting responses, and why his significance has come to be judged in such strikingly different ways at different times, it is necessary to examine the remarkable variety of subsequent contexts in which his work has in fact been viewed.

i

We can be reasonably confident that the initial reaction to Ferguson's work was indeed overwhelmingly positive among the British literary and intellectual elite of the day. This happy situation was beautifully captured in two famous letters which have survived, from Hume in London to Ferguson in Edinburgh, informing him, in obviously congratulatory terms, of the favourable reception that the newly-published *Essay* was then receiving from the great and the good in the metropolis. The first communication, dated 24 February 1767, reports that

> I happen'd yesterday to visit a person three hours after a Copy of your Performance was open'd for the first time in London. It was by Lord Mansfield. I accept the Omen of its future Success. He was extremely pleas'd with it; said it was perfectly well wrote; assured me, that he woud not stop a moment till he had finish'd it, and recommended it Strongly to the Perusal of the Archbishop of Yorke, who was present. (C I:71)

The second missive, on 10 March, permitted Hume to continue on the same pleasing theme:

> It is with a sincere Pleasure I inform you of the general Success of your Book. I had almost said universal success; and the Expression wou'd have been proper, as far as a Book can be suppos'd to be diffus'd in a Fortnight, amidst this Hurry of Politics and Faction. I may safely say that I have met with no body, that has read it, who does not praise it; and these are the people, who by their Reputation and Rank commonly give the Tone on these Occasions. Lord Mansfield encreases his Style of Approbation; and is very loud to that Purpose in his Sundays Societies. I heard Lord Chesterfield and Lord Lyttelton express the same sentiments; and what is above all, Cadell, I am told, is very happy; and is already projecting a second edition of the same Quarto Size. (C I:72–3)

This was praise indeed. We may suppose that Hume's sketch deliberately flattered a good friend who was not always quite as self-confident as his majestic prose might sometimes have suggested. But it also appears to have been a fair appraisal of the typical response among those whose opinions would most have mattered to Ferguson. For from powerful and well-placed men like Mansfield (Perthshire-born Lord Chief Justice of

England), the Archbishop of York (Robert Hay Drummond, yet another Perthshire Scot advantageously positioned in the English establishment) and both Chesterfield and Lyttelton (leading politicians, literary patrons and authors in their own right), professions of real satisfaction with Ferguson's intellectual achievement inevitably carried natural authority. We can also be sure, incidentally, that the expressions of delight from Thomas Cadell (Ferguson's publisher) were unfeigned: in 1768 there promptly appeared the second edition about which Hume was already speculating encouragingly.

Public attitudes, meanwhile, seem to have reflected the evident support for Ferguson from such distinguished authorities, as well as being further influenced by the opinion-forming reviewers who sought to convey to a widening literate population of British readers and book-buyers the definitive judgments of the *cognoscenti*. Indeed, in this, the first great age of literary journalism and criticism, Ferguson was the recipient of more than his fair share of unrestrained commendation. The *Critical Review*, for example, among the most eminent of national journals, left its great army of individual readers in no doubt as to the tangible personal benefits that they might each derive from exposure to Ferguson's newly-published *Essay*: 'none can sit down to the perusal of it', the *Critical* gushed in 1767, 'without rising a better man and citizen, or without finding himself improved in sense, sentiment, and stile'. It was 'one of the few modern compositions which unites preciseness of reasoning and depth of judgment, to an uncommon elegance of diction', and would speak directly to 'readers of every other denomination'. A remarkably similar judgment was promulgated in the rival *Monthly Review* that same year, whose critic asserted, with equal certainty that his opinion would help mould the attitudes and behaviour of a discriminating public, that the *Essay* would be found useful by 'every reader of taste'. In the *Town and Country Magazine*, meanwhile, another journal with an extensive readership throughout England, the *Institutes* were promoted in 1770 as 'a valuable compendium for use of the students of the college of Edinburgh, and... a work worthy of their attention'.

Further support for the rapid rise of Ferguson's star in the British literary firmament was provided by the preparedness of contemporary reviewers to go to great lengths to heighten awareness of the intellectual content of certain books. In effect, reviewers increasingly shouldered the burden of supplying their own readers with convenient summaries of important new texts. In the *Gentleman's Magazine*, for example, the most influential of all British magazines at this period, Ferguson's work was substantially explained as well as praised: 'He observes also, that "art" itself is "natural" to man…', reported one contributor in 1767 on the celebrated first section of Part I of the *Essay*, before going on to underline that 'the work is strongly recommended to our readers. It abounds with subtile thought, ingenious sentiment, & extensive knowledge, and is written with a force, elegance, and perspicuity, seldom found in modern performances'. In much the same vein, the substance of the *Institutes* received particularly helpful exposure in the pages of *The Scots Magazine* in November 1769. This widely-read Edinburgh-based journal offered a list of the work's miscellaneous contents as well as some choice excerpts from the text, doubtless intended to whet the book-buying appetites of its own discerning clientele.

Yet beyond the manipulative reach of the great literary periodicals, which consciously strove to shape the judgments of the wider public as the ultimate consumers of texts, the immediate private reactions of Ferguson's own Scottish circle, and of the wider community of active theorists and other authors, also seem to have been overwhelmingly positive. Smith's attitude towards the *Essay* is predictably regarded as by far the most important, given the broad similarities but also the intriguing contrasts between this work and the *The Wealth of Nations*. Indeed, much interest has come to surround the embarrassing spat between the two old friends, late in Smith's life, which is sometimes believed to have arisen over the latter's belated accusation that Ferguson had stolen substantial parts of his analysis of the division of labour from what he must have known about the content of Smith's own Glasgow lectures: certainly when Ferguson reported Smith's death in 1790 to Sir John Macpherson, he confessed that 'matters as you know were a little awkward when he was in health'; and later "Jupiter" Carlyle, in his wonderfully gossipy memoirs, claimed that 'Smith had been weak enough to accuse him of Having Borrowed some of his Inventions without owning them. This Ferguson Denied, but own'd he Deriv'd many Notions from a French author and that Smith had been there before him' (C I: 341; A 144). Yet it is clear that Smith and Ferguson had continued to enjoy harmonious relations during almost all of the more than two decades since the first appearance of the *Essay*—at least until Smith's health and mood simultaneously declined. Nor is there any other evidence to link the undoubted awkwardness between the old friends during the late 1780s with a specific charge of plagiarism. Moreover, we know that Ferguson himself was hugely admiring of the *The Wealth of Nations* when it appeared in 1776, since he informed Smith in April of that year 'You are surely to reign alone on these subjects, to form the opinions, and I hope to govern at least the coming generations' (C I:142). All that it seems safe to conclude, therefore, is that the two Adams were cordially supportive of one another's philosophical work, even if some disagreement on individual points of interpretation (as was in fact the norm between all of the Scottish Enlightenment's leading figures) remained inevitable from time to time.

From Ferguson's other immediate friends and associates, in Scotland and elsewhere, the responses to his work, even when privately expressed and away from Ferguson's hearing, invariably fell somewhere between unambiguous favour and fanatical over-enthusiasm. This was especially true of the *Essay*, about which Lord Kames, for example, wrote effusively to Elizabeth Montagu in 1767, 'to recommend to you a book lately published here... This subject, not less beautiful than interesting, employs some vigour in writing, and much original thought...' (C II:546). Mrs Montagu, for her part, was at least as eager in her praise for Ferguson's first work, clearly enraptured by his adept interweaving of acute moral observation and nostalgic classicism: 'I approve extremely of Mr Fergusson', she simpered, 'in the preference he gives to the magnanimous virtues, above the effeminate and luxurious arts of modern life; and wish he could infuse into us some of the Spartan spirit he admires so justly' (C II:547). James Boswell, young Edinburgh lawyer and aspiring man of letters, was another fervent admirer of Ferguson's *Essay*—calling it 'a pretty Book' (CJB 168)—, whilst his friend, the Devon minister William Temple, normally a sober as well as particularly well-informed judge of the Scottish Enlightenment's key publications, wrote back to Boswell with an astonishingly fulsome encomium in January 1768 on first 'reading Mr Ferguson's book':

What a monument of penetration, of patriotism, of genius & of eloquence! What a beautiful lecture to form young men to honour & great actions. If I ever have a son & he does not adore the author of that book, I'll disinherit him as a bastard & a stranger to my blood. (CJB 221)

In Europe, meanwhile, the leading philosophers of the day seem to have been no less sincerely impressed with Ferguson's achievement.

d'Holbach, for example, hailed it, in a letter to Ferguson which has survived, as 'answering completely to the high opinions I had conceived
of your great abilities and ingenuity...', whilst Voltaire, whom it will be
remembered Ferguson actually met in 1774 during a Continental tour,
had the opportunity to flatter him to his face, as the slightly bemused
guest at Ferney subsequently related to Carlyle, for having 'civilized the
Russians'—this last observation usually being interpreted as an allusion
to the rapid incorporation of Ferguson's *Institutes* into the curriculum of
the University of Moscow (C I:77, 124).

What was very widely true of the *Essay*'s early reception among those
contemporaries who were regarded as being best qualified to judge
was also usually true of their responses to the *History* in due course.
John Logan, for example, Scottish clergyman and minor man of letters, was perhaps typical in his ardour, writing to the Edinburgh-born
historian and Grub Street journalist Gilbert Stuart—himself no friend
of the Moderate clergy—in praise of the *History* on its first appearance
in 1783:

Dr Ferguson's Roman History hath been advertised. The pomp and glitter; the
point & antithesis; and all the tawdry and meretricious ornaments which mark
and disgrace some popular historians, he avoids and disdains. He writes History
with the simplicity and dignity of an Old Roman... (C II:575)

Although we may be sure that Ferguson would have been delighted
with being thought an 'Old Roman', this assessment is otherwise by no
means easy to accept at face value: after all, whatever the many merits
of Ferguson's writing, a gift for plainness was never remotely amongst
them. But Logan, who would in 1786 advise his friend Carlyle of the
fact that the French translation of the *History* had also been 'exceed-
ingly well received at Paris', does at least preserve some of the genuine
enthusiasm with which many contemporary arbiters, their dispositions
formed by a shared love of classicism and increasing nervousness about
Britain's potential for mirroring the fate of the ancient republics, were
always likely to receive Ferguson's successive publications (C II:575).
Lord Jeffrey, an early nineteenth-century Scots lawyer and politician
who, as a young Edinburgh student in the late 1780s, had narrowly
missed the chance to sit mesmerised at the feet of the recently-retired
Ferguson, was also typical of this reaction in his own assessment of the
History, for a later edition of which he even subsequently composed a
eulogistic preface: 'it has been justly described', boasted Jeffrey, 'as one

which not only delights by the clearness of its narrative and the boldness of its descriptions, but instructs and animates by profound and masterly delineations of character, as well as by the philosophical precision with which it traces the connection of events' (H iv).

Despite this welter of admiration, however, contemporaries, and even those who knew Ferguson personally, could never quite manage complete unanimity on his merits as a philosopher and historian. In fact, Hume's private reservations are much the best known, even though the precise reasons for his dislike of the *Essay* in particular have, unfortunately, not come down to us. The evidence points, though, to Hume's disapproval being rooted as much in differences of temperament and style as in substance. For, as we have repeatedly seen, Ferguson's writing, in all four of his published works, was sententious and declamatory to a fault—written, as Queen Victoria later alleged of Gladstone's tone during royal audiences, as though he were addressing a public meeting. We also know that this high-flown oratorical style was not to everyone's taste, even at a time when classical rhetoric was still greatly admired. Blair, another friend and a well-regarded authority on literary manner, was surely right when he observed that Ferguson's writing in the *Essay* was exceptionally 'rousing and animating', whilst Henry Mackenzie, the doyen of the Scottish Enlightenment's novelists, probably had a point when alleging (though, tactfully, only in private correspondence with a third party) that it was actually 'pompous' and 'bombastic': given these reactions even among sympathisers, it seems likely that Hume too might well have found Ferguson's purple prose indigestibly rich (E xvii; C II:575). But Hume almost certainly had additional reservations. Chief among these is likely to have been the intense moral fervour with which Ferguson approached the study of mankind: it would not be entirely misleading to say that whereas Ferguson was pre-occupied with the urgent promotion of public virtue, his texts as a result reading very often like a lecture, or even a sermon, Hume was, by contrast, emollience personified, concerned with offering perceptive observations and, particularly in his essays and historical writing, providing his readers with more than a modicum of agreeable entertainment. It is therefore easy to imagine Hume's growing exasperation as his eyes fell upon the insistent pleading and urgent exhortations that litter Ferguson's prose. Like Lord Kames, who had candidly dismissed the *Institutes* as 'a careless trifle intended for his scholars and never meant to wander out of that circle', Hume may well have regarded Ferguson's *Essay* as savouring too much of the classroom or the pulpit to meet the rather different requirements of modern polite literature (ASSP 97).

There were also, however, points of interpretation on which it is difficult to see Hume having been wholly comfortable with his friend's idiosyncratic contribution to the "Science of Man". In particular, we know that neither Hume nor Smith shared Ferguson's obsessive faith in the continuing efficacy of volunteer citizen militias, even though both were members of the Poker Club and largely avoided public disagreement with their friends among the Moderate clergy on this touchstone question of Scottish national honour. At bottom, it is clear that they doubted the wisdom, in what was plainly an age of ever-increasing occupational specialisation, accelerating technological change, and worldwide warfare on land and sea, of imagining that a part-time, localized force of public-spirited amateurs could reasonably still serve as a viable means of national defence: 'there I must be against you', acknowledged Ferguson in that otherwise flattering letter to Smith on the publication of the *The Wealth of Nations*, in which the latter's scepticism about militias had been clearly signalled in the remark that they 'must always be much inferior to a well disciplined and well exercised standing army' (C I:143; WN II:302). More widely, however, arising fundamentally out of this same preparedness, which he very much shared with Smith, to prioritise the lessons of modern political economy over those of ancient moral philosophy, it seems likely that Hume's comparative optimism about the prospects for modern society would also have been a significant aggravating factor as he formulated his considered private response to Ferguson's *Essay*.

Ferguson, as we have seen, argued that the combined effects of politeness and commerce posed a serious threat to traditional public spirit and so to the essential political vitality of eighteenth-century states. Hume, however, regarded commerce as overwhelmingly beneficial and politeness as the most likely resource in modern times for maintaining political liberty: by learning how to converse with intelligence and elegance, and to behave in a moderate and tolerant manner, it was possible, Hume thought, for his contemporaries to shore up their hard-won freedom and prosperity. From this basic dichotomy between the two friends almost certainly followed a further source of tension that the publication of the *Essay* could only have exacerbated. Ferguson, as we know, actually welcomed a degree of factionalism and turbulence because they presented rare additional opportunities in modern monarchies for active participation by a concerned and committed citizenry: politeness, by this reckoning, worked in a manner directly contrary to the public interest because it tended effectively to suppress, or at least to counteract, the enhanced vigour and virtue that internal conflict would otherwise stimulate. Hume, meanwhile, considered faction, even in modern societies, in far more straightforward terms, merely as a source of potentially fatal division and instability: on this reading, politeness was in fact a useful cultural restraint, acting as a brake upon the damaging centrifugal impulses of the disparate individuals and groups who comprised a complex commercial society. Clearly, with such profound and wide-ranging differences in their social and political philosophies, Hume's reservations about Ferguson's ideas, in whatever form they were actually expressed, ought not to have been too surprising.

Nor, if Carlyle's recollections are completely accurate, was the *History* always quite so rapturously received by Ferguson's contemporaries in the mid-1780s as the *Essay* had been by his Edinburgh circle, Hume apart, in the later 1760s. According to Carlyle, whilst he and some of the author's other close friends 'could not refrain from saying that Ferguson's was the best history of Rome', some in Scotland by this time were apparently less convinced, 'taking every opportunity to undermine the reputation of Ferguson's book' (A 231). Carlyle elsewhere alleged that anti-Scottish sentiments lay behind some of the English disapproval of the *History*; that it also suffered in comparison with the incomparable work of Gibbon, then only partially complete but already the dominant force in contemporary classical scholarship, seems certain (A 283–4). Another observer, sadly unidentifiable, left some additional hints as to the causes of the book's somewhat cool reception in certain quarters:

Ferguson has given the world lately an important Work, a History of the Rise and Fall of the Roman Republic. Of this there are different opinions; but the most prevalent is rather not so high as the former character of the author would have led people to form. He has treated his subject rather in a Narrative than in a reflective way, & has been sparing of those general & philosophic views of the subject which is the great distinction between Modern History, since the time of Montesquieu & the ancient'. (K 78–9)

Clearly, then, not all contemporaries, even in the Scottish capital itself, were uncritical of Ferguson's intellectual and literary achievements. Indeed, in the case of the *History* in particular, its dense and stately narrative might well have failed to capture the imaginations of a fashion-conscious readership in the mid-1780s, who, their historical tastes insensibly modified by exposure to a growing tribe of saccharine sentimentalists (led by Gilbert Stuart, who promoted the view that history's 'weeping eye is the indication of an instructive sorrow'), might well have found Ferguson's haughty and orotund political didacticism less appealing than previously (HSER I:202). It may well be significant, therefore, that an exploration of much the most intriguing aspect of Ferguson's contemporary reception would require us to look not to Edinburgh, nor to England, nor even to France, but to Germany. For it was here that a peculiar kind of Enlightenment—the *Aufklärung*—had burst into life. And it was here, it transpired, that Ferguson's works, and the remarkable blend of ideas and arguments they contained, would register their most extensive, but also their most perplexing, impact.

ii

Late eighteenth-century Germany was in fact gripped by what became known as *Anglophilie*—a mania for Britain in general and for British literature in particular. But within this general process, which was itself an important element in the formation of Germany's own Enlightenment, the appreciation of Scotland's particular contribution to modern thought was also a prominent feature: 'Who would not respect the Scots Ferguson, Smith, Stewart, Millar, Blair?', inquired Johann Gottfried von Herder, the great philosopher and folklorist, revealing clearly the deference towards the leading Scottish thinkers which he and his contemporaries invariably felt it necessary to exhibit (TE 57). German admiration for the Scottish Enlightenment inevitably led on to concerted efforts at the translation and local publication of its major works. Yet as has recently been pointed out by Fania Oz-Salzberger, who has made this subject very much her own, the practical business of translating the Scottish theorists, and of doing so in a form appropriate to the needs and expectations of German-speaking readers, was actually far from straightforward. Indeed, Ferguson's work may well represent the outstanding example of the complexities, and the potential pitfalls, involved. For the *Essay*, translated not particularly well by Christian Friedrich Jünger in 1768, was long overshadowed in the estimation of German audiences by the *Institutes*, which received brilliant translation in 1772 at the expert hands of Christian Garve. At the same time, the stereotypical eighteenth-century German reader's own preference for literary, educational and philosophical literature over political and social analysis may have tended further to reduce the initial German profile of the *Essay* in comparison with Ferguson's primarily pedagogical work (TE 62).

Problems with the international, cross-cultural transmission of Enlightenment texts also affected Ferguson's German reception in other unexpected ways. In particular, even as they learned to read and increasingly to appreciate his work, German-speakers tended to reserve their greatest enthusiasm for those aspects of Ferguson's thought that seemed most apposite in their own distinctive social and political circumstances. For example, Isaak Iselin, the celebrated Swiss lawyer and historian, made sure to include glowing references to Ferguson in *Versuch über die gesellige Ordnung* (1772), his own account of man's undeviating ascent towards moral perfection. In the process, however, Iselin neatly ignored the *Essay*'s less-than-helpful speculations about the essential reversibility of progress and the ever-present danger of corruption: such selectivity was in fact to become a familiar approach to the interpretation of Ferguson's philosophy, reflecting peculiar preconceptions about history that were unique to the *Aufklärung* (TE 169–89). At the same time, the tendency to read Ferguson in the light of their own assumptions also meant that German-speakers were inclined to overlook or downplay those aspects of his work which made sense only in relation to a Scottish or British context: for example, his republican concerns with participatory citizenship and his fixation with the problems of commercial society attracted less attention than they had from Ferguson's English-speaking audiences. On the other hand, because of some superficial similarities with Reid and Beattie, in so far as he too could be usefully employed as a bulwark against both Hume's scepticism and the worrying inroads being made by the French materialist philosophers, Ferguson tended to be identified routinely in Germany as one of the leading British proponents of the "Common Sense" theory of perception—even though, as we have seen, whilst this was certainly a significant part of the intellectual background to Ferguson's moral philosophy, it was by no means a question to which he had made a particularly original contribution.

A further problem in relation to the extraordinary German enthusiasm for Ferguson's work was the way in which the very process of translation from English into German substantially affected the presentation of his arguments, and so also the impression of Ferguson's intellectual significance that many foreign readers were able to form. Here Garve is probably the best example, not least because of his emphasis upon the Ferguson of the *Institutes*—which is to say, upon Ferguson as moral philosopher and teacher rather than as political philosopher and historian. But Garve's translation of this work, rendering Ferguson's value-laden English terminology into equally but often very differently value-laden German, had the remarkable additional effect of changing the nature and implications of the ideas that were conveyed. For example, the phrase 'public spirit', so common in all of Ferguson's discussions, is variously translated in the German version of the *Institutes*, but on occasion actually becomes *Vaterlandsliebe*, a word certainly full of local resonance but also failing to convey the evocative mixture of classical republican and English overtones that congregated so densely in Ferguson's original text. By a similar method, utilising familiar German terms whose connotations were emphatically not those intended by Ferguson, Garve frequently preferred variations on *der Staat* (implying essentially the political institutions of government) where the original text had made deliberately broader reference, again very much in the republican mould, to the political realm and the public sphere. Even more revealing, perhaps, Garve, who like Iselin and many of the thinkers of the German Enlightenment was engrossed in a belief in man's stately progress towards a higher condition of moral perfection, tended to translate Ferguson's prose in such a way as to make the *Institutes* seem considerably more supportive of this notion than Ferguson could ever have imagined: Ferguson's straightforward 'excellence', for example, is given greater strength and resonance by Garve by being translated as *Vollkommenheit* (in German, 'completeness' or even 'perfection'), whilst even mere 'improvement', another key noun in Ferguson's English text, is made far more momentous (implying advancement towards perfection) when rendered in German as *Annäherung an... [die] Vollkommenheit* (TE 190–216).

As a result of processes of this kind—in which it should be added that Garve was by no means the only or the worst offender—Ferguson's ability to convey his own distinctive ideas accurately in the context of the German Enlightenment was greatly affected. Rather, it would be fairer to say that his writings were frequently associated with a series of alternative philosophical causes, to at least some of which Ferguson himself would never willingly have subscribed. Ferguson's conditional, open-ended and non-deterministic vision of man's history, for example, was a far cry from the perfectibilism of the *Aufklärung*, but this inconvenient fact did not stop his impressive philosophical profile in Germany from being exploited in such a way as to popularise this particular theory. On the other hand, civic humanism was unquestionably a central part of his self-conscious dialogue with other British theorists like Harrington, Fletcher and Smith, and was also significant for his understanding of the peculiar operations of the Hanoverian constitution and of Britain's current experience of rapid commercialisation. Such concerns in turn made republican citizenship a characteristic—arguably *the* characteristic—trope of Ferguson's political philosophy. Yet this often spoke confusingly, even unintelligibly, to Ferguson's admirers overseas, and therefore positively invited inaccurate or downright misleading translation: Iselin's preference for rendering 'activity', perhaps the most pregnant noun in all of Ferguson's vocabulary, as *Bestreben* (indicating striving, but without any political or public-oriented connotations at all), was typical of what German insensitivity to the specific calls of republicanism could do to their understanding and appreciation of Ferguson's work. If nothing else, therefore, the extraordinary story of Ferguson's prominence in the *Aufklärung* is a salutary reminder that the transmission, interpretation and absorption of philosophical ideas sometimes takes them surprisingly far from the original meanings and purposes which their author intended.

iii

Momentous shifts within the essentially alien landscape of German philosophy were also to provide the impetus for such posthumous interest as Ferguson's ideas were still to attract by the middle decades of the nineteenth century. For, along with his friend Smith, Ferguson would emerge as a comparatively minor though explictly-acknowledged part of the intellectual baggage with which Marx and Engels laboured heroically to establish the principles of historical materialism and, in due course, the philosophy and political economy of communism. Yet here again, learning the lessons afforded by Ferguson's somewhat careless treatment at the hands of the German Enlightenment, it is necessary for us to continue to be aware of the considerable violence to the original meaning and implications of his thought that de-contextualised interpretations of his writings were capable of inflicting in the highly-distinctive German philosophical environment. In fact, such caution seems all the more nec-

essary in the light of what also turns out to be an exceptionally complicated pattern of intellectual transmission between mid-eighteenth-century Edinburgh philosophers and Continental socialist ideologues in the
era of the 1848 revolutions. Indeed, with recognisably Scottish ideas not
only directly shaping the development of Marxism but also being mediated indirectly through the seminal but notoriously obscure writings of
Georg Wilhelm Friedrich Hegel, in relation to this most problematical
phase of Ferguson's unanticipated posthumous career as an influential
theorist neither clarity nor consensus are easy to arrive at.

   With Hegel, a towering name in the history of European philosophy
even if it were not for his unwitting starring role as the inspiration to
Karl Marx, it is clear at least that Ferguson was a significant formative
influence. Partly this was because during his own education the young
and impressionable Hegel was exposed, at the height of *Anglomanie*, to
the writings of Ferguson, Smith, Hume and the other Scottish theorists: it is known, for example, that he devoured the *Institutes* in Garve's
classic early translation, and that he subsequently pored over the *Essay*.
Partly this was also because Hegel was strongly influenced in his own
philosophical development by some of Ferguson's principal admirers
of the preceding generation: these included Garve himself, Friedrich
Heinrich Jacobi (who was actually unusual in Germany in the extent of
his straightforward absorption of Ferguson's participatory republicanism) and Friedrich Schiller (a major poet of the *Aufklärung* and, in his
early years, very much shaped by the mainstream interpretation—or,
as we have seen, misinterpretation—of Ferguson's political philosophy).
Scholars have therefore not been at all surprised to find specific allusions
to Ferguson's writings in Hegel's own densely-argued works. One of the
most suggestive instances arises, for example, in the two philosophers'
respective treatments of the social fragmentation which follows on from
the division of labour: in insisting that 'The absolute bond of the people, namely ethical principle, has vanished, and the people is dissolved',
Hegel certainly appears to regurgitate the essence of Ferguson's famous
claim in the *Essay* that the progressive separation of the professions tends
naturally 'to break the bonds of society' (SEHA 227).

   Indeed, it was one of the critical implications of Ferguson's treatment
of the division of labour that Hegel most famously assimilated into his
own highly-original analysis of man's historical development. This was
the notion of the individual's alienation from his own community, by
which Ferguson, still thinking analytically as a republican political theo-

rist and, significantly, using constructions such as 'lose the sense of every connection' and 'no longer apprehend the common ties of society' rather than the word 'alienation' as such, had sought to explain the undesirable consequences of functional specialisation (E 208). In fact, in Ferguson's account, what came in the nineteenth century to be known as 'alienation' was the essentially psychological and moral outcome of a process which, in the natural pursuit of economic gain, had rendered individuals increasingly unable even to comprehend, let alone to share, the common interests of their fellow men. Ultimately, in terms guaranteed to send shivers down the spines of the republican-minded, this development had seemingly made redundant such hitherto-crucial social values as selfless patriotism and concern for the common good.

In Hegel's treatment, particularly in the *Phenomenology of Mind* (1807), the process of alienation, or, strictly speaking, *Selbstentfremdung* (to which the English 'self-estrangement' actually comes rather closer in meaning), operates in a recognisably similar way, as a consequence of man's progress through history. But it also takes on rather more positive overtones, largely because of Hegel's very different conception of history. In effect, in Hegel's hands alienation is now to be understood as an inevitable aspect of man's progressive development towards the final state of complete self-consciousness and self-realisation. Such eventual destinations for human progress reveal once again Hegel's many points of contact with *Aufklärung* perfectibilism. But they should also remind us of the alarming ease with which certain aspects of Ferguson's ideas were instinctively (and sometimes unconsciously) re-worked by German-speaking readers so as to accord with their own essentially deterministic, one-directional vision of man's evolution.

It was in turn from Hegel, as much as from Ferguson directly, that Marx, especially in his younger and more humanistic phase, was to borrow the concept of man's progressive alienation through history—although, significantly, Marx allowed it in the process to re-acquire far less attractive connotations. Indeed, particularly in what have later become known as the *Economic and Philosophical Manuscripts of 1844*, alienation has a central role to play in Marx's analysis of the immense damage wrought within society and to the human character itself—especially that of the labourer—by the disorienting and disabling experience of commercial relations. Yet terminological discrepancies, expressing underlying conceptual differences, make it hard for us to be certain about the precise nature of Marx's indebtedness to Ferguson. Above all, it is distinctly awkward that, in Marx's version, alienation takes on a variety of guises. In one sense it manifests itself as estrangement (or *Entfremdung*) from one's community—a notion perhaps suggesting something reasonably close to Ferguson's original conception. But it also serves, usefully for Marx's emerging critique of capitalism though far less obviously related to anything that Ferguson had imagined, as a process (now labelled *Entäusserung*) by which the individual is himself transformed into a saleable object or commodity, thereby losing touch with an important aspect of his previous social humanity. And it involves in still other instances what is sometimes rendered in English as 'reification' (in the German, *Vergegenständlichung*), a notion, as well as a word, completely foreign to the discourse of the Scottish Enlightenment and which means something akin to the effective mutation of the work or economic use-fulness of an individual person into a material object. Given these wide divergences in both meaning and implication, it should be clear that the road between Ferguson and Marx on the subject of alienation is in reality anything but straight and narrow.

It also becomes obvious on closer inspection of Marx's own writings that his famously-acknowledged debt to Ferguson as an analyst of com-mercial society, rendered explicit at several points in *Capital* (1867), is far from easy to interpret. Ferguson's observation, for example, in the section of the *Essay* dealing with 'the Separation of Arts and Professions', that, in manufacturing contexts, the enterprise appears to 'prosper most, where the mind is least consulted, and where the workshop may, with-out any great effort of imagination, be considered as an engine, the parts of which are men', is quoted verbatim in the first volume of *Capital* (E 174; CM I:341). But for Marx these words merely provide a use-ful remark with which to embellish his own hostile account of capital-ist productive activity—a form of analysis, based on the class relation-ship between employers and workers, that Ferguson clearly could never have imagined. An even more illuminating example of Marx's evident genius for manipulative quotation arises out of Ferguson's observation that, whilst the military commander is 'occupied in the conduct of dis-ciplined armies' where he 'may practise on a larger scale, all the arts of preservation, of deception, and of stratagem, which the savage exerts in leading a small party, or merely in defending himself', the ordinary sol-dier, engaged directly in fighting, and performing only local and limited tasks, 'is confined to a few motions of the hand and the foot'. In fact, rather than incorporating the *Essay*'s complete discussion of the respective experiences of generals and infantrymen, only Ferguson's pithy single-sentence summary—'The former may have gained, what the latter has lost'—actually finds its way into *Capital* (E 175; CM I:341n). More curiously still, it is re-deployed by Marx as a direct quotation in illustration of a quite different point, this time about the contrast between employers and employees. In other words, by a shameless act of predatory decontextualisation, Marx manages completely to obscure the specifically military application (and also the powerful republican resonances) of Ferguson's original argument whilst providing himself with a seemingly apt observation from an authoritative eighteenth-century source that would reinforce his own denunciation of the exploitative relationship between capitalists and labourers.

We even need to treat Marx's categorical insistence upon Ferguson's significance in the development of his own political economy and social analysis with a sizeable pinch of salt. After all, Marx was apparently unaware of the existence of Smith's Glasgow lectures. Even more remarkably, he seems to have formed the bizarre impression that Smith had been, as is notoriously asserted on three separate occasions in *Capital*, 'a pupil of A. Ferguson' (CM I:124, 334, 342). As a result, Marx must be regarded as, at best, untrustworthy on the vexed question of the precise intellectual lineage of the nineteenth-century theorists among the writers of the Scottish Enlightenment. Yet it remains true that Marx was at least on solid ground when arguing that Ferguson in particular had pointed out with unusual vehemence the moral dangers that specialisation potentially presented in modern times: Ferguson's extensive treatment of alienation, however differently-construed from those of his later admirers, was certainly an important new departure in social philosophy. Nor would it be sensible for us simply to dismiss the familiar claim that Ferguson was a pioneering contributor to the foundation of a broader analytical method—in effect, to sociology in the making—which sought to explain the evolution of mankind by reference to a succession of discrete stages of human development.

As we have seen, a version of this type of social analysis, dividing man's history into the three stages of 'savage', 'barbarous' and 'polished', was indeed an integral feature of Ferguson's historical thought. This was never, of course, as relentlessly deterministic as Marx's subsequent account of society's progress towards the dictatorship of the proletariat. Nor was it as fixated upon the material causes and characteristics of social change as Smith's political economy, or, for that matter, as Marx's histor-

ical materialism: after all, other and older categories of analysis continued their hold on Ferguson's imagination, strongly influencing his own
judgments and preventing any possibility of his being able to present an
account of man's history shorn of a moral philosopher's fascination with
manners and mores or a classical historian's overt republican prejudices.
At the same time, however, Ferguson did make an important contribution to the Scottish Enlightenment's theoretical achievement. In particular, he brought a distinctive mixture of issues, concerns and perspectives
to the evolving discussion of human society that colleagues like Smith
and Robertson, and even Hume, could never have offered. Such things,
being irrelevant to Marx's wholly different analytical agenda, which went
on to prescribe the terms of debate for most social theorists for most
of the next hundred-and-fifty years, were inevitably overlooked, or at
least seriously under-estimated, by the comparatively few later readers
who bothered to consult Ferguson's works. Indeed, by the turn of the
twentieth century, Ferguson's role had largely been reduced to that of a
quarry, not necessarily to be treated with any great care or respect, for
the occasional mining of fragments which might help illuminate some
of the more obscure quotations and footnotes in *Capital*.

iv

Only in the middle decades of the twentieth century did there finally
begin to occur a substantial revival of interest in Ferguson's achievements as a philosopher in his own right. Much more readily identified
in retrospect, this unexpected development was essentially a reflection of
shifting intellectual fashions among academics and modern theorists of
society. The most important of these trends for Ferguson's renewed stature was probably the emergence of self-conscious interest among social
scientists in the historical origins of their own disciplines: long dimly
aware that psychology, behavioural science, anthropology, political science and, most of all, sociology and economics, had discernible roots in
the Enlightenment, modern practitioners in Britain and North America,
perhaps emboldened by the increasing importance of those disciplines
in the academic curriculum, at last began to want to know more about
the earliest expressions of their own characteristic inquiries and modes of
thought. It was in this process, at times seeming more like an exercise in
intellectual genealogy—which is to say, seeking principally to establish

a clear lineal relationship between eighteenth-century ideas and twentieth-century preoccupations—that Ferguson began steadily to assume far
greater prominence.

The modern re-discovery of Ferguson as a 'founding father of social
science'—to use one telling phrase, originating in the late nineteenth
century, that had become current by the 1960s—cannot itself be
divorced from the specific investigation of the eighteenth-century roots
of Marxism (AF 17–26). For the marginal contributions to historical
materialism made by Ferguson's analysis of social development, and the
seemingly more significant assistance afforded by his treatment of the
individual's experience of social atomisation, ensured that any attempt
to reconstruct Marxism's complex pre-history would be obliged to make
space at least for a proper consideration of the Scottish Enlightenment.
Certainly this particular view of Ferguson's significance was to be central to the interest shown in him by several mid-twentieth-century
scholars. These included Roy Pascal and, particularly, Ronald Meek, a
New Zealand-born historian of economic theory, for whom a thorough
understanding of the Scottish stadialists appeared increasingly important in explaining the Enlightenment origins of the classical Marxist
analysis of human history which, especially aggressively in Meek's case,
they themselves still avowed.

Although in terms of an economically-determined theory of social
evolution it was plainly Smith who mattered most, in other respects it
was Ferguson who now began to appear a singularly useful inspiration for
the early Marxists. Smith had obviously supplied the truly rigorous and
systematic explanation of the division of labour; but it was Ferguson, as
we have seen, who had actually issued the lengthier and more strongly-
worded warnings about its moral and social consequences. Both of these
eighteenth-century Scottish professors, or so it seemed, had therefore
helped create a new and important way of thinking about man's development from which Marx himself had subsequently taken his cue: even
if unwittingly, they had indubitably originated, Meek claimed in one
particularly unguarded phrase, '*a*, if not *the*, materialist conception of
history' (ST 19). In the same vein, in his influential monograph *Social
Science and the Ignoble Savage* (1976) Meek was willing to number
Ferguson among a coherent group of path-breaking proto-Marxist mate-
rialists whose intellectual fascination with primitive peoples, and whose
urgent need to explain the rapid economic changes that were even then
overtaking Scottish society, had led them to devise a fully-formed theory

of social evolution in which the characteristic conception of property was the chief determinant of that society's stage of development. Such inquiries, claimed Meek, could safely be regarded as 'one of the first important exercises in the field which modern sociologists have marked out as their own' (SSIS 150).

At the same time, however, very different readings of Ferguson—as, even more commonly, of Smith—had begun to suggest by the 1960s that it was actually the inter-connecting techniques and assumptions of historical writing and social theory that had emerged in eighteenth-century Scotland which most deserved careful reappraisal. Indeed, in this light, the "Science of Man" now appeared a strikingly early exploration of the rich possibilities that might exist for constructing a coherent and scientifically-rigorous study of man in all of his many social guises. A key contribution to this dawning realisation of the methodological importance of the Scottish Enlightenment theorists was undoubtedly the work of the American scholar William C. Lehmann, whose *Adam Ferguson and the Beginnings of Modern Sociology* (1930) is still the foundation of all modern Ferguson scholarship in English. Declaring himself fascinated by 'the utter modernity of Ferguson's viewpoint', Lehmann, who later also published revealing studies of Kames and Millar, made a powerful case for identifying in Ferguson's carefully-structured exposition of general laws or principles of human development the rudiments of an essentially sociological approach, in which the evolving institutions, practices and even cultural values of particular societies could be explained in terms of their direct relationship with specific social and economic circumstances (L 7). Another American academic, Gladys Bryson, in her pioneering *Man and Society: The Scottish Enquiry of the Eighteenth Century* (1945), similarly provided a wider perspective in which Ferguson's remarkable originality as a systematic investigator of early human society could be understood alongside the parallel work of his close friends: 'Probably no other group of thinkers before the twentieth century', she concluded, 'so self-consciously set about encompassing a whole range of discussion which now has become highly elaborated and parceled out among the several social sciences' (MS 239). From these important beginnings a number of more recent scholars have been able to assess the relative input to nineteenth-century sociology that may actually have been made by Ferguson in particular: John D. Brewer, for example, more recently claimed nothing less than that 'Ferguson marks the point where sociological discourse on the structure of society begins to emerge out of the discourse of civic humanism and conjectural history' (CH 26).

Alongside this growing interest in the origins of economics and sociology, recent scholarship has also shown itself increasingly fascinated by the potential for interpreting Ferguson as a major contributor to the subsequent formation of other academic disciplines which, strictly speaking, did not exist at the time of the Scottish Enlightenment. Not surprisingly, Ferguson's work as a historian, which, as we saw, was especially innovative and radical, has been particularly intriguing to those scholars interested primarily in the theory and practice of modern historiography. Conjectural history, and not least the possibility of employing evidence from known societies so as to fill in the gaps in our understanding of unknown but stadially-identical societies, has proved an especially thought-provoking aspect of Ferguson's work. Indeed, in an important study by Harro Höpfl entitled 'From Savage to Scotsman: Conjectural History in the Scottish Enlightenment', it has been argued that Ferguson's (as well as Smith's) thought represented a remarkable advance in the development of the historical method, effectively bridging the gap between the conventional narrative history of the past and the emergence of fully-fledged social analysis in the future. The theory of unintended consequences has also earned the concerted attention of Ronald Hamowy, who has presented this important feature of the Scottish Enlightenment's innovative approach to history as having opened up the space to develop a plausible historically-grounded philosophy based on the irregularity, unpredictability and essential irrationality of social change: this was, asserts Hamowy, 'perhaps the single most significant sociological contribution made by that group of writers whom we today regard as constituting the Scottish Enlightenment' (TSO 3). Surprisingly, however, there has been little interest in Ferguson's *History* (no edition of which has appeared since the final American printing in 1861): it is thus the Ferguson of the *Essay* who has so far dominated recent thinking about his methodological legacy to historians.

A further dimension to this essentially genealogical approach to Ferguson, and again tending to portray his work fundamentally as an unusually far-sighted anticipation of later intellectual developments, has been the interest of certain political economists in some of the wide-ranging ideological implications of his ideas. It is in this light that, although clearly taking a secondary role to Smith, Ferguson has become an established fixture in what has been presented by some scholars, par-

ticularly in the United States, as the Scottish Enlightenment's committed advocacy of limited government and economic liberalism in modern
societies. This is not, of course, a completely straightforward interpretative manoeuvre. As we know, Ferguson was in his own day a vocal opponent of the American Revolution and a sceptical observer of domestic
constitutional reform. At the same time, his commitment to the vocabulary of civic humanism, with its provocative claims about moral corruption and incurable paranoia about any threat to public spirit and social
cohesion, also poses problems for any account seeking to present him as
a natural ally of unregulated commerce or possessive individualism.

   Yet it remains true that Ferguson's political theory, especially in the
Essay, is far more sympathetic to the aspirations of the citizen (however
narrowly conceived this category in practice was) than to the pretensions
of government. Indeed, the whole tenor of his thinking is sceptical about
the proposition that granting further powers and additional resources
to a class of superintending professional politicians will increase rather
than jeopardise the meaningful freedoms and material prosperity which
were slowly carved out by previous generations. As a result, Ferguson's
writings, buttressed intellectually by the theory of unintended consequences and reinforced at a personal level by his lifelong allegiance to
the pragmatic compromise which was the eighteenth-century British
constitution, are profoundly hostile to that line of idealistic political
rationalism which, running from his contemporaries among the radical
constitutional reformers, through his immediate Marxist successors and
on eventually to the twentieth-century advocates of all-embracing government, insists that the state and its far-sighted legislators are the most
likely source of earthly salvation. In essence, Ferguson saw the individual
citizen—with his (and, in Ferguson's vision, it was certainly always *his*,
not her) interacting complex of materialistic and social passions—as the
best guarantor of his own liberty, as well as the most appropriate agent
by which the worthwhile ambitions of humanity in general could be
progressed.

   As a consequence of this powerful vision, to which Ferguson, as we
have seen, devoted some of the highest-flown passages of rhetoric in
the *Essay* and the *Principles*, it has proved much too tempting for late-
twentieth-century neo-conservative political theorists and economic lib-
erals not to co-opt Ferguson for their own purposes—even if this has
meant that his equally fluent observations about the moral implications
of the division of labour and the unrestrained pursuit of private profit

have tended to receive short shrift. Friedrich Hayek, for example, the influential Austrian-born theorist whose work was inspirational in the emergence of explicitly free-market-oriented governments from the late 1970s, made much use of Ferguson and Smith. Indeed, his considerable admiration for Ferguson's insights was highlighted by his selection of an adaptation of a key phrase borrowed from the *Essay*—'The Results of Human Action but not of Human Design'—as the title for his own definitive discussion of the theory of unintended consequences. Hayek, like Sir Karl Popper, whose critique of deterministic thinking under the heading 'the poverty of historicism' was equally seminal in the emergence of the New Right, also found unintended consequences, in very much the form deployed by Ferguson, an extremely effective polemical weapon. In particular, it helped Popper and his disciples to construct a philosophically coherent explanation for the manifest failures of centralised planning and the state ownership of industries which had assumed such prominence in economic policy not only in Eastern Europe but even in Britain and many other parts of Western Europe in the decades after the Second World War.

One final strand of Ferguson's thought has, however, stimulated even greater recent excitement about its potential contemporary applicability. And this too, like Ferguson's slightly surreal identification as a remote forerunner of Thatcherite economic liberalism, involves the proposition that, especially in the *Essay*, he can in fact be interpreted as contributing something directly relevant and meaningful to current debates about the nature of modern society. This claim revolves in particular around the allegedly momentous significance of Ferguson's conception of what he chose to call 'civil society'. But even the initial task—that of determining what Ferguson may actually have intended us to understand by his periodic use of this pregnant phrase—turns out to be surprisingly hazardous. Indeed, the quest for clarity on this point must lead us eventually back to the very purposes for which the *Essay* was written, and, to a great extent, to the provocation originally offered by Rousseau's remarkable notion of a pre-social state of nature. For this, as we saw, is ultimately why Ferguson, in those compelling early pages of the *Essay*, sketches out his seductive account of a structured and coherent form of human community which has been gradually coming into existence from a remote era in history. Initially, then, and throughout much of the remainder of the book, 'civil society' is not really very much more than Ferguson's preferred name for a longstanding and absolutely necessary expression of man's nature. In fact, that the term so obviously implied in Ferguson's mind an elastic and encompassing vision of man's social existence in many different ages and places—thereby creating more than enough conceptual space to accommodate the otherwise disparate themes with which he was going to be concerned—was doubtless an important consideration in his decision to incorporate it without further qualification in the title of the *Essay*.

The belief that Ferguson's conception of 'civil society' is directly relevant to a better understanding of our own social circumstances at the turn of the twenty-first century, however, ignores one inconvenient fact. For it is very easy to demonstrate that the modern debate on 'civil society' has deviated in a number of crucial respects from Ferguson's original eighteenth-century analysis. By far the most significant disjunction in the evolving argument about the essential characteristics of something conveniently described as 'civil society' arises once again out of critical divergences between Ferguson's richly evocative English terminology and what have come to be accepted as the appropriate German synonyms. In particular, it is unfortunate that the equivalent term, *bürgerliche Gesellschaft*—itself a rendering of the Latin *societas civilis* first popularised by Pufendorf's translators and then subsequently favoured by that clear majority of the leading modern theorists of 'civil society' who happen to have been native German-speakers—brings inescapably with it into the discussion a series of implications and associations that are virtually impossible to reconcile with the assumptions embedded in Ferguson's preferred English formulation. Not least, it is of great importance to the subsequent development of the concept that *bürgerliche Gesellschaft*, even among Ferguson's German contemporaries, referred only to a relationship binding a society of free and equal individuals together into a political community: by no means would this term have suggested to German ears the much broader subject with which so much of the *Essay* is in fact concerned, namely a society in its wider public (and often non-political) manifestations.

Yet this was to be only the beginning of a fateful linguistic divergence. For subsequently, the same German phrase came to be understood, particularly through the influence of Immanuel Kant in his *Groundwork of the Metaphysics of Morals* (1785) and Hegel in the *Philosophy of Right* (1821), as signifying a political society of people which was also conceived as being entirely separate from the formal institution of the state (*der Staat*). Neither of these evolving usages, it goes without saying, connotes the much more extensive communal arena, including the spheres of politics, government and commerce, but also much else besides, that Ferguson's expansive discussion had plainly sought to accommodate. Even more importantly, however, for differentiating it from the successive layers of meanings with which Ferguson's use of the English term was so fruitfully loaded, the equivalent German terminology was devoid of any republican connotation of active political participation by citizens. Indeed, with resonances even less congruent with Ferguson's discussion of 'civil society' in the *Essay*, the preference of many modern commentators for a variant English translation—particularly tempting, it appears, given the adoption and strongly pejorative use of *bürgerliche Gesellschaft* by Marx and Engels in *The German Ideology* (1845–6)—has given us the even more heavily-loaded and un-republican formulation 'bourgeois society'. This is also, as will be obvious, an utterly un-Fergusonian phrase, in which socio-economic class takes centre-stage and in which the phenomenon is in any case by implication confined to the present commercial or capitalist era.

The necessarily complex business of translation (and re-translation) between the major European languages is, however, responsible for only part of the problem involved in making sense of the supposed significance of Ferguson's original discussion among those later analysts of our social experience who have chosen to summon up the notion of 'civil society'. Indeed, to complicate matters even further, Ferguson himself appears occasionally to have used the phrase 'civil society' in subtly different and rather more restricted senses from that which the title of the *Essay* and much of his book's discussion seem to assume. Once, for example, Ferguson refers explicitly to what he calls 'the dignities, and even the offices, of civil society', thereby hinting, perhaps, that 'civil' society might after all be strictly coterminous with 'political' society—a crucial semantic shift that would evidently bring Ferguson at least momentarily closer to the conception later popularised by Kant and Hegel (E 79). In a number of other instances, however, Ferguson employs the phrase so that it appears virtually synonymous with 'refined' or 'polished', suggesting in effect that 'civil society' might, after all, be a condition limited to the higher stages of social progress: in Part V of the *Essay*, for example, we hear of 'the ruinous corruptions to which nations are liable, in the supposed condition of accomplished civility' (E 199). This usage too might appear to contain at least a limited anticipation of the subsequent Marxist analysis, in so far as 'civility' is now evidently confined to the

more advanced phases in man's historical development. It will be clear,
though, that the preoccupation here with human behaviour rather than
with class relations, as well as the perceptible nervousness about the
reversibility of progress, make even this feature of Ferguson's analysis
really only a very distant cousin to the later socialist critique of 'bourgeois society'.

Plainly, any attempt to make strong connections between Ferguson's
conception of civil society and the work of later theorists in this field
runs the risk not only of over-reliance upon highly-selective quotation
but also of inviting charges of outright mis-representation of his arguments. It is in this light that we need to approach the evidence that
many recent participants in this debate have in fact chosen to conceptu-
alise civil society in such a way that it clearly refers to something quite
different again—essentially, the extensive realm of associational activity
lying specifically beyond the reach of the state and the formal political sphere with which Ferguson himself had been so much concerned.
In other words, following neither the *Essay*, nor even Hegel or Marx,
but, if anything, the example of the French political writer Alexis de
Tocqueville, whose *Democracy in America* (1835) suggested that the
complex inter-personal networks generated by voluntary activities had
helped to create America's peculiarly strong attachment to democratic
values, civil society has come to be most often been presented in the last
fifty years as the space that arises between the individual and the state.
It is a sphere, therefore, in which private citizens choose to engage freely
with one another, independently of the functioning of government or
the immediate business of political and legal administration.

For some theorists, such as Robert Nozick, the American author
of *Anarchy, State and Utopia* (1974), civil society, conceived also as
embodying the innumerable market transactions between people that
are necessary in a commercial age, becomes effectively an alternative to
the authority of the state, and so an argument for the withdrawal of the
government from anything beyond a small core of unavoidable respon-
sibilities: ultimately, this takes us back to a position not far from that
proposed, albeit with more explicit borrowings from Ferguson, by advocates of liberal economics like Hayek. Not surprisingly, however, other
variations on the theme of the associational conception of civil society
have had even greater attractions to those observers for whom the unfree
states of Eastern Europe, or the authoritarian regimes of Latin America,
or simply the imperfections of the modern capitalist system, have served

as the major spur to theorisation. It is therefore no coincidence that the Polish dissident Adam Michnik, the democratic Czech leaders Václav Havel and Václav Klaus, and in Britain the Czech-born theorist Ernest Gellner, have each in different ways spoken of the flourishing of civil society as an effective counterweight to the crushing embrace of the Marxist-Leninist state: Gellner's thought-provoking book *Conditions of Liberty: Civil Society and its Rivals* (1995), for example, contains a heartfelt plea for voluntary associationalism as the surest and soundest foundation of freedom, and, though again there must be a suspicion that it benefits from a somewhat strained interpretation of the *Essay*'s arguments in the round, quotes approvingly from Ferguson's account of civil society, which Gellner elsewhere suggests explicitly would 'help throw light on contemporary issues connected with this notion' (AFSR 119).

From a quite different ideological perspective it has also been European intellectuals like the Italian theorist Antonio Gramsci and the German social scientist Jürgen Habermas, both of them mainly concerned with activities independent either of the state or of capitalism, who have made the most compelling cases for individuals and groups to occupy an identifiable 'public sphere' which is not only non-governmental but also non-commercial in character. In this account, of course, it is not traders and entrepreneurs in the marketplace—much less the patriotic citizenry actively running every aspect of public life, as envisaged by Ferguson—who are seen as the quintessential embodiment of civil society. It is rather the earnest members of trade unions and those involved in organisations campaigning for causes such as nuclear disarmament or environmentalism. Yet each of these associational visions, with their partial echoes of Hegel's counterposing of *bürgerliche Gesellschaft* and *der Staat*, are also substantially different from the notion of an all-encompassing single arena of public participation that sustained Ferguson's thinking about society, just as they abandon—indeed frequently excoriate—the impoverished classical Marxist notion of civil society as an economically-defined space created specifically for bourgeois endeavour.

Nor, however, should we be entirely surprised by the scale of these intellectual disjunctions, even if they have been partially masked by the extent to which theorists over the last fifty years have tended ritually to invoke Ferguson's name in their own support. For we need always to remember that, from his lofty vantage-point in the Scottish Enlightenment, Ferguson himself was actually looking back to the Roman republic rather than forwards to the twentieth century. He knew nothing of—and, we may be sure, would have cared even less for—the representative mass democracy and global commercialism to which we have now become accustomed. Far less could Ferguson be expected to have anticipated the unique social and psychological constraints upon people's liberties and identities imposed by modern totalitarianism, against which his words have been so often quoted (and, as we have already seen, frequently mis-interpreted). This, as much as anything else, should tell us why Ferguson's conception of civil society, grounded as it is in classical republican notions of direct participation in all forms of public activity by every member of a supremely energetic (but always narrowly-defined) male citizenry, inevitably bears at most only a passing resemblance to the theories of civil society that have attracted such attention among politicians and philosophers in recent decades.

iv

Given the extraordinarily varied points of entry taken by those interested in excavating and re-interpreting Ferguson's thought as a valuable insight into a diversity of modern concerns, it is all the more surprising that there have been so few attempts by historians to explore his work in the round. Indeed, David Kettler's *The Social and Political Thought of Adam Ferguson* (1965) remains the outstanding modern treatment of Ferguson's ideas; but it is actually the only book-length study to have been ventured since Lehmann's in the 1930s, and is also unique in its willingness to base an assessment of Ferguson's entire intellectual project on a close study of the distinctive environment of eighteenth-century Scotland. As Kettler argues, the interest of virtually all other scholars in seeing Ferguson either as a pioneer of sociological methods, or as an exponent of classical political economy, or as a visionary theorist of civil society, has tended, albeit unintentionally, to involve 'doing some violence to the integrity of Ferguson's total production' (K 4). It is also difficult, when the aim is manifestly to render eighteenth-century arguments relevant to distinctively contemporary preoccupations, to appreciate what an Enlightenment philosopher like Ferguson was really doing—particularly if this also involves a failure to appreciate what Kettler identified as the 'issues which excited his generation', as well as the peculiar local conditions in which those concerns had emerged (K 4). This is why renewed fascination with the Scottish Enlightenment as a whole in recent years has been such a useful development for anyone interested in making sense of Ferguson's work not as a partial anticipation of later innovations but genuinely *on its own terms*. For in greatly increasing our historical understanding of the social and cultural worlds Ferguson inhabited, and in which he thought and wrote, it is a potentially vital addition to our appreciation of his ideas, their derivation and their original significance.

Although the circumstances surrounding the birth of the modern study of the Scottish Enlightenment remain mildly controversial among specialists, there is no doubt that by the late 1960s it had acquired real momentum, with academic historians and philosophers at work constructing a much more sophisticated and nuanced account of the distinctive Scottish contribution to eighteenth-century European civilization. For our own purposes, however, it is significant that, both as a thinker in his own right and as an integral part of the Edinburgh-based cultural community forming the creative core of the Enlightenment in Scotland, Ferguson was perhaps the individual who gained most in relative standing. Taken together with the parallel interest in putting Ferguson's ideas to work in a growing number of anachronistic contexts, the recent scholarly preoccupation with the Scottish Enlightenment clearly played its part in triggering the extraordinary rash of modern editions of the *Essay* which have appeared, and even the reprinting in facsimile of editions of the *Institutes* and the *Principles*. Less tangibly but even more importantly, these processes also effectively restored Ferguson to an intellectual status, and a sheer luminosity in the history of ideas, that he had perhaps not enjoyed—and certainly not in his native Britain—since the closing decades of the eighteenth century.

Above all, our steadily-improving understanding of the Scottish Enlightenment has made it possible to see aspects of the "Science of Man", to return to Hume's much-quoted description of his friends' philosophical mission, with a clarity and a resolution that was long absent. In particular, its implicit claim to coherence, and to the existence of a unifying intellectual project, has been rendered that much more convincing. With what we increasingly know about Smith, Robertson, Millar, Kames and Hume, as well as the preoccupations and peculiarities of the minor Scottish theorists, Ferguson's declaration in the *Institutes* that he was compiling a 'natural history of man' reverberates in all sorts of new ways (I 16–17). Indeed, the latter begins to seem like the only appropriate encapsulation of those necessarily intertwined inquiries about man's existence—biological, environmental, psychological and cultural, as we might subsequently want to assign them to our own separate categories—which together, as the constituent parts of a single enterprise, were assumed at the time to comprise the legitimate business of the aspiring modern philosopher.

It is in this context, too, that we better understand the scientific assumptions informing the writing and teaching of a person in Ferguson's position. For the empirical bias of the "Science of Man", and its continual emphasis upon observation and experiment as necessary preconditons to the formulation of a satisfactory explanation, were critical. This was precisely what made Ferguson such an extraordinarily active collector of historical information—of data, as we might now say—as well as an enthusiastic analyst and interpreter of what he had gathered: hence, of course, Ferguson's blunt determination in the *Principles* that, in studying man, we should only 'collect facts, and endeavour to conceive his nature as it actually is, or has actually been, apart from any notion of ideal perfection, or defect' (P I:1). In fact, the Scottish Enlightenment's obsession with the prestigious experimental methods of Bacon and Newton—the latter 'the incomparable metaphysician and geometrician', according to Ferguson's colleague, Walter Anderson, a Berwickshire clergyman and minor classical historian—explains much about the remarkable junction of history, philosophy and social theory that we find in Ferguson's writings, as in that of so many of his contemporaries and friends (PAG 465). If Smith, according to Millar, was 'the Newton of political economy', then Ferguson too was a pioneer in leading the study of mankind along the trail blazed so brilliantly for the study of the non-human world by the mathematicians and physical scientists (HVEG II:429–30n).

Other features also come into sharper focus as we begin to understand more about the distinctive fault-lines in eighteenth-century Scotland. Not only those characteristics which Ferguson shared with his colleagues but even his striking idiosyncracies as a thinker start to make much more sense. Greater appreciation of the social and cultural fissures in Scottish society—not least those widening gaps between the Highlands and the Lowlands—allows us to appreciate, for example, the full significance of Ferguson's commitment to a relatively open-ended and non-deterministic account of human progress (even if his later German and Marxist disciples were to be guilty of mis-representing this crucial part of his work). Awareness of Ferguson's contemporary Scottish circumstances also forces us to take full measure of the limitations which that context imposed upon his judgments. After all, as well as being an Edinburgh academic with a growing international reputation, Ferguson was also a man who had been born into a Gaelic-speaking community and who was especially proud to have served his country in arms. Given this background, and the fact that it enabled Ferguson to view the accumulated evidence of man's long history from what, for an intellectual, was even in this period a relatively unusual perspective, it ought to be less surprising that he found it so hard to accept that modern society—particularly when it was characterised by rampant commerce, creeping professionalisation, and a sometimes insipid attachment to politeness—was superior in every respect to simpler social forms, in which communal ties, martial vigour and public spirit all seemed rather easier to sustain. On the somewhat discouraging historical evidence that Ferguson tended to focus upon, why would such an ambiguous process of advancement not also be intrinsically prone to reverse? Indeed, might it not be the case that the eventual fragmentation and political eclipse of an advanced society—just like Rome in antiquity—were the perfectly natural consequences of its increasingly materialistic priorities and accelerating moral decline? Modern interpretations which see Ferguson's deep interest in primitive peoples, and particularly his nostalgic empathy with certain aspects of their existence, as a reflection of his own roots in the more traditional social system of the Scottish Highlands which during his own lifetime was in the process of being finally obliterated by the rampaging forces of commerce and civility, are, despite their apparent simplicity, not necessarily all that far wide of the mark.

Indeed, in the light of what our greater understanding of the world of the Scottish Enlightenment can apparently tell us about Adam Ferguson, it is tempting also to ask how far a better appreciation of Adam Ferguson and his philosophical career might assist us in deepening our understanding of the character of the Scottish Enlightenment. Nor is this mere idle speculation. For the desire to see the essential characteristics of an era's high culture embodied in one major writer or thinker is well-attested: the "Age of Shakespeare" is gratingly familiar; the notion of an "Age of Johnson" has much appeal among historians of mid-eighteenth-century England. With Scotland in the same period, this is clearly a more difficult game to play. Because of his scepticism in particular, Hume, the most celebrated figure then and now, is too untypical to serve as a satisfactory symbol. Smith, whose own views, though more cleverly disguised, may not have been too dissimilar, might well be ruled out on the same basis. Robertson, whose published contribution was largely confined to historiography, is simply too narrow in compass. Millar and Blair fall at the same hurdle. Kames, recognised even by his friends as strictly *sui generis*, cannot even be considered.

But Ferguson, at least, has merit. Above all, his motivating concerns as historian, moral philosopher, social theorist and political thinker seem to have included many of the principal currents coursing through educated Scottish society during his lifetime. Perplexed by the threat to religion from scepticism, to morality from politeness, to liberty from tyranny and self-interest, and to social cohesion and nationhood from commerce and corruption, Ferguson in fact represented like few other men the breadth but also the distinctive essentials of Scotland's elite culture in the age of the Enlightenment: as Gladys Bryson noticed, 'It can with truth be said that the set of ideas dealt with by Ferguson was representative of his Scottish contemporaries' (MS 52). His most singular quality, nevertheless, remained his capacity for articulating those widespread anxieties in a wholly characteristic style, for exploring the implications of modernity as they seemed to him to impact upon the world around him. This cannot, despite what many of his later admirers have rashly proposed, make him our contemporary, able to tell us how to live in our own time. But it is sufficient to make Adam Ferguson, a man who encapsulated the world of the Scottish Enlightenment better than any of its other major thinkers, worthy of our continuing respect as one of the most remarkable and inventive thinkers that Scotland has produced.

A Guide to Further Reading

As we have already seen, particularly in Chapter 6, the history of Ferguson scholarship since his lifetime has been extremely chequered, and the resulting body of literature suffers from a number of unhelpful biasses. Above all, far too much has appeared in the twentieth century which seeks to cast Ferguson as the intellectual progenitor of the modern sociologist, political economist or social theorist. By contrast, a disappointingly small proportion of the work, at least until very recently, has focused on Ferguson as a moral philosopher and university teacher active in eighteenth-century Scotland. It is clearly, however, in this latter perspective that Ferguson needs to be approached if we are fully to understand his work and its historical significance.

For background information on the man and his life, the basic source, written at a time when a few people could probably still remember Ferguson from personal acquaintance, is John Small, 'Biographical Sketch of Adam Ferguson, L.L.D. and F.R.S.E., Professor of Moral Philosophy in the University of Edinburgh', *Transactions of the Royal Society of Edinburgh*, 23 (1862–4), 599–665. One of the two key twentieth-century treatments of Ferguson's philosophical work is also essential for biographical purposes: David Kettler, *Social and Political Thought of Adam Ferguson* (Columbus, OH: Ohio State University Press, 1965). An extended biographical treatment by Jane Bush Fagg provides a substantial introduction to *The Correspondence of Adam Ferguson*, Vincent Merolle (ed.), 2 vols (London: Pickering & Chatto, 1995) and, since it makes extensive use of Ferguson's own letters, published as a set for the first time, is also strongly recommended. The reminscences of Henry Cockburn's boyhood contained in *Memorials of His Time* (Edinburgh: Adam and Charles Black, 1856) provide some of the most striking anecdotes of Ferguson and his friends in their old age.

It is a remarkable fact that, at least in relation to the literature in English, just two major works represent the basis of all serious subsequent understanding of Ferguson's philosophy. These should be sought out by anyone interested in pursuing this subject further. Kettler's in particular is an outstanding work of intellectual biography and shows no imminent signs of being superseded in its analysis of Ferguson's thought. Indeed, its reading of Ferguson's motivation and peculiarities as a thinker is exemplary, and it goes farther than any other treatment towards situating him in the world of the Scottish Enlightenment. It suffers, however,

Adam Ferguson

from the characteristic problem of all genuinely trail-blazing academic studies. For Kettler actually succeeded brilliantly in showing how other parts of the hitherto-uncharted territory which was eighteenth-century Scottish cultural and intellectual life might fruitfully be explored. Unfortunately, other scholars have gone on to publish so much in this broader field, not least inspired by Kettler's pioneering work, that many aspects of his book not directly concerned with Ferguson's intellectual development now appear effectively outmoded.

The other foundational work, W.C. Lehmann's *Adam Ferguson and the Beginnings of Modern Sociology* (New York and London: Columbia University Press, 1930), is more obviously dated in its techniques and, as its title makes only too plain, is concerned with presenting certain aspects of Ferguson's social thought and methodology as a contribution to the later development of the social sciences. For all its transparent anachronism, however, this analysis has been very influential in making Ferguson's work seem both readily accessible and more directly relevant to a modern academic audience. Among those subsequent works exploring Ferguson primarily as an iconic theorist of social change who had a formative impact on nineteenth- and twentieth-century thinkers, the account offered in Ronald Meek's *Social Science and the Ignoble Savage* (Cambridge: Cambridge University Press, 1976) is a particularly important example, with its ambitious attempt to link Ferguson (and, of course, Smith) with the later Marxist tradition.

In recent years there have nevertheless been a number of more plausible and historically sensitive interpretations which see Ferguson's philosophical career as a reflection of distinctively Scottish and Enlightenment preoccupations and which also show genuine interest in the disparate contemporary contexts in which his achievements were first established and evaluated. Fania Oz-Salzberger's marvellous *Translating the Enlightenment: Scottish Civic Discourse in Eighteenth-Century Germany* (Oxford: Clarendon Press, 1995) is a model of how to study the impact of thinkers as a strictly historical phenomenon, with its revelation that Ferguson, like several of his immediate Scottish friends, was frequently misunderstood, or even misrepresented, by his many German admirers. At the same time, her recent edition of the *Essay on the History of Civil Society* (Cambridge: Cambridge University Press, 1995) is an admirable introduction to Ferguson's most famous work, containing a short biography as well as a fine survey of the *Essay's* principal features: still very much available in the bookshops, it is also the edition on which, with the reader's convenience in mind, my own quotations and referencing have drawn. The first modern edition, however, edited by the late Duncan Forbes (Edinburgh: Edinburgh University Press, 1966), also remains invaluable, being prefaced with a thoughtful and balanced introduction to Ferguson's philosophy from one of the most influential modern students of the Scottish Enlightenment.

Several important studies of specific aspects of Ferguson's life and activities have appeared in recent years and these will provide useful points of departure for further reading. The key study of Ferguson's inter-locking academic and clerical *milieux* is Richard B. Sher, *Church and University in the Scottish Enlightenment: The Moderate Literati of Edinburgh* (Princeton, NJ: Princeton University Press, 1985). Sher's exploration of the dispute over Ossian between Ferguson and Thomas Percy is also a fascinating study in eighteenth-century literary combat: 'Percy, Shaw, and the Ferguson "Cheat"; National Prejudice in the Ossian Wars', in Howard Gaskill (ed.), *Ossian Revisited* (Edinburgh: Edinburgh University Press, 1991), pp. 204–45. The related controversy over the Scots militia, and Ferguson's central role in its conduct, is covered in John Robertson, *The Scottish Enlightenment and the Militia Issue* (Edinburgh: John Donald, 1985), while Sher has also contributed a careful examination of the intellectual tensions that this question raised amongst his circle of close friends: 'Adam Ferguson, Adam Smith, and the Problem of National Defense', *Journal of Modern History*, 61 (1989), 240–68.

Finally, if it is through a writer's own words that we can best come to know him, it is worth emphasising the value of reading Ferguson's works themselves. Inevitably, the *Essay* is much the best-served by modern editions which are not only readily accessible but also still in print: apart from the two already noted, the edition by Louis Schneider (New Brunswick, NJ, and London: Transaction Publishers, 1980) is also interesting, even though, apart from a new introduction, its text is the same as Forbes'. The *Institutes* have also recently benefited from a re-print of the original 1769 edition (London: Routledge/Thoemmes Press, 1994) which, though an expensive volume and presented without any introduction or critical apparatus, is a very welcome development. Re-prints of the *Principles* appeared in 1973 (New York: AMS Press) and 1978 (New York: Garland). Thus far we still lack a modern edition of the *History*; though, in the light of growing interest in Ferguson, it seems likely that we will not have too long to wait.

Bibliography

1. Works of Adam Ferguson

An Essay on the History of Civil Society, (ed.) Duncan Forbes (Edinburgh: Edinburgh University Press, 1966)

An Essay on the History of Civil Society, (ed.) Fania Oz-Salzberger (Cambridge: Cambridge University Press, 1995)

The History of the Progress and Termination of the Roman Republic (New York: J.C. Derby, 1856)

Institutes of Moral Philosophy (London: Routledge/Thoemmes Press, 1994)

Principles of Moral and Political Science, 2 vols (London: A. Strahan and T. Cadell, and Edinburgh: W. Creech, 1795)

Reflections Previous to the Establishment of a Militia (London: R. and J. Dodsley, 1756)

Remarks on a Pamphlet lately Published by Dr. Price... (London: T. Cadell, 1776)

The Correspondence of Adam Ferguson, (ed.) Vincent Merolle, 2 vols (London: Pickering & Chatto, 1995)

2. Other works of the Scottish Enlightenment

Adams, John, *Curious Thoughts on the History of Man* (Dublin, 1790)

Anderson, Walter, *The Philosophy of Ancient Greece* (Edinburgh, 1791)

Arnot, Hugo, *The History of Edinburgh* (Edinburgh, 1779)

Balfour, James, *A Delineation of the Nature and Obligation of Morality* (Edinburgh, 1763)

Belfour, John, *A New History of Scotland* (London, 1770)

Blackwell, Thomas, *An Enquiry into the Life and Writings of Homer* (London, 1735)

Boswell, James, *The Correspondence of James Boswell and William Johnson Temple, 1756–1795: Volume 1: 1756–1777*, (ed.) Thomas Crawford (New Haven: Yale University Press, 1997)

Carlyle, Alexander, *Autobiography*, 3rd edition, (ed.) J. H. Burton (Edinburgh: William Blackwood, 1861)

Carlyle, Alexander, *The Question Relating to a Scots Militia Considered* (Edinburgh, 1760)

Cockburn, Henry, *Memorials of His Time* (Edinburgh: Adam and Charles Black, 1856)

Dalrymple, Sir John, *Memoirs of Great Britain and Ireland*, 2 vols (Edinburgh, 1771

Dunbar, James, *Essays on the History of Man in Rude and Uncultivated Ages* (Dublin, 1782)

Fletcher, Andrew, *A Discourse Concerning Militia's and Standing Armies* (London, 1697)

Forbes, Duncan, 'Thoughts on Religion, Natural and Revealed', in *Works of Duncan Forbes of Culloden* (Edinburgh, 1755)

Gillies, John, *The Orations of Lysias and Isocrates* (London, 1778)

Grant, James, *Essays on the Origin of Society* (Edinburgh, 1785)

Hume, David, *Enquiries Concerning Human Understanding and Concerning the Principles of Morals*, (ed.) P. H. Nidditch, 3rd edition (Oxford: Oxford University Press, 1975)

Hume, David, *Letters*, (ed.) G. Birkbeck-Hill (Oxford: Clarendon Press, 1888)

Hume, David, *A Treatise of Human Nature*, (ed.) P.H. Nidditch, 2nd edition (Oxford: Oxford University Press, 1978)

Hutcheson, Francis, *Enquiry into the Original of our Ideas of Beauty and Virtue* (London, 1725),

Kames, Lord, *Historical Law Tracts*, 2 vols (Edinburgh, 1758)

Kames, Lord, *Sketches of the History of Man*, 2 vols (Edinburgh, 1774)

Millar, John, *An Historical View of the English Government*, 4 vols (London, 1812)

Millar, John, *The Origin of the Distinction of Ranks* (London, 1771)

Robertson, William, *The History of Scotland* (London, 1759)

Smith, Adam, *Essays on Philosophical Subjects*, (ed.) W. Wightman (Indianapolis: Liberty Press, 1982)

Smith, Adam, *The Theory of Moral Sentiments* (London, 1759)

Smith, Adam, *The Wealth of Nations*, 2 vols (London, 1776)

Stephen, Sir Leslie, *History of English Thought in the Eighteenth Century*, 3rd edition (New York, 1949)

Stewart, Dugald, 'Dissertation Exhibiting a General View of the Progress of Metaphysical, Ethical, and Political Philosophy, Since the Revival of Letters in Europe', *Supplement to the 4th, 5th and 6th Editions of the Encyclopaedia Britannica* (Edinburgh, 1815–24)

Stuart, Gilbert, *The History of Scotland from the Establishment of the Reformation Till the Death of Queen Mary*, 2 vols (London, 1782)

Stuart, Gilbert, *View of Society in Europe in its Progress from Rudeness to Refinement* (Edinburgh, 1778)

Turnbull, George, *Observations upon Liberal Education* (London, 1742)

Turnbull, George, *A Treatise on Ancient Painting* (London, 1740)

Tytler, Alexander, *Plan and Outline of a Course of Lectures on Universal History, Ancient and Modern* (Edinburgh, 1782)

3. Other studies

Brewer, John D., 'Adam Ferguson and the Theme of Exploitation', in *British Journal of Sociology*, 37 (1986), 461–78

Brewer, John D., 'Conjectural History, Sociology and Social Change in Eighteenth-Century Scotland: Adam Ferguson and the Division of Labour', in D. McCrone, S. Kendrick and P. Straw (eds.), *The Making of Scotland: Nation, Culture and Social Change* (Edinburgh: Edinburgh University Press, 1989), pp. 13–30

Brewer, John D., 'The Scottish Enlightenment', in A. Reeves (ed.), *Modern Theories of Exploitation* (London and Beverly Hills: Sage, 1987), pp. 6–29

Bryson, Gladys, *Man and Society: The Scottish Enquiry of the Eighteenth Century* (Princeton, NJ: Princeton University Press, 1945)

Clausewitz, Karl von, *On War*, (ed. and tr.) Michael Howard and Peter Paret (Princeton, NJ: Princeton University Press, 1989)

Gellner, Ernest, 'Adam Ferguson and the Surprising Robustness of Civil Society', in his and César Cansino (eds.), *Liberalism in Modern Times* (Budapest and London: Central European University Press, 1996), pp. 119–131

Graham, H.G., *Scottish Men of Letters in the Eighteenth Century* (London: Adam and Charles Black, 1908)

Hamowy, Ronald, *The Scottish Enlightenment and the Theory of Spontaneous Order* (Carbondale: Southern Illinois University Press, 1987)

Hayek, F.A., *Studies in Philosophy, Politics and Economics* (Chicago: University of Chicago Press, 1969)

Höpfl, H., 'From Savage to Scotsman: Conjectural History in the Scottish Enlightenment', *Journal of British Studies*, 17 (1978), 19–40

Kettler, David, *Social and Political Thought of Adam Ferguson* (Columbus, OH: Ohio State University Press, 1965)

Lehmann, W.C., *Adam Ferguson and the Beginnings of Modern Sociology* (New York and London: Columbia University Press, 1930)

Locke, John, *Two Treatises of Government* (ed.) Peter Laslett (Cambridge: Cambridge University Press, 1988)

MacRae, D.G., 'Adam Ferguson, 1723–1816', in Timothy Raison (ed.), *The Founding Fathers of Social Science* (Harmondsworth: Penguin, 1963)

Marx, Karl, *Capital*, 3 vols (London: Lawrence & Wishart, 1977)

Meek, Ronald, 'The Scottish Contribution to Marxist Sociology', in J. Saville (ed.), *Democracy and the Labour Movement* (London: Chapman and Hall, 1954), pp. 84–102

Meek, Ronald, 'Smith, Turgot, and the "Four Stages" Theory', in his *Smith, Marx and After: Ten Essays in the Development of Economic Thought* (London: Chapman and Hall, 1977), pp. 18–32

Meek, Ronald, *Social Science and the Ignoble Savage* (Cambridge: Cambridge University Press, 1976)

Oz-Salzberger, Fania, *Translating the Enlightenment: Scottish Civic Discourse in Eighteenth-Century Germany* (Oxford: Clarendon Press, 1995)

Oz-Salzberger, Fania, 'Adam Ferguson's Histories in Germany: English Liberty, Scottish Vigour and German Rigour', in Benedikt Stuchtey and Peter Wende, (eds.), *British and German Historiography, 1750–1950* (Oxford: Oxford University Press, 2000), pp. 49–66

Oz-Salzberger, Fania, 'From Male Citizen to Neuter Mensch: the Emasculation of Adam Ferguson's Civic Discourse by the German Enlightenment', *Eighteenth-Century Scottish Studies*, 7 (1993), 5–8

Pascal, Roy, 'Property and Society: The Scottish Historical School of the Eighteenth Century', *Modern Quarterly*, 2 (1938), 167–79

Pope, Alexander, *An Essay on Man*, (ed.) Maynard Mack (London: Methuen, 1950)

Robertson, John, *The Scottish Enlightenment and the Militia Issue* (Edinburgh: John Donald, 1985)

Rousseau, Jean-Jacques, *Du Contrat Social*, (ed.) Ronald Grimsley (Oxford: Clarendon, 1972)

Scott, W. R., *Adam Smith as Student and Professor* (Glasgow: Jackson, Son and Company, 1937)

Sher, Richard B., 'Adam Ferguson, Adam Smith, and the Problem of National Defense', *Journal of Modern History*, 61 (1989), 240–68

Sher, Richard B., *Church and University in the Scottish Enlightenment: The Moderate Literati of Edinburgh* (Princeton, NJ: Princeton University Press, 1985)

Sher, Richard B., 'Percy, Shaw, and the Ferguson "Cheat"; National Prejudice in the Ossian Wars', in Howard Gaskill (ed.), *Ossian Revisited* (Edinburgh: Edinburgh University Press, 1991), pp. 204–45

Small, John, 'Biographical Sketch of Adam Ferguson, L.L.D. and F.R.S.E., Professor of Moral Philosophy in the University of Edinburgh', *Transactions of the Royal Society of Edinburgh*, 23 (1862–4), 599–665

Swingewood, Alan, 'Origins of Sociology: The Case of the Scottish Enlightenment', *British Journal of Sociology*, 21 (1970), 164–80

Waszek, Norbert, *The Scottish Enlightenment and Hegel's Account of 'Civil Society'* (Dordrecht: Kluwer Academic Publishers, 1988)

Index

relations with Scotland, 2-3, 10-11, 71

environment 42, 58-9, 66, 148

Epictetus, 22, 36, 37, 38

epistemology, 25-8, 129

Europe, history of, 72, 76

Fagg, Jane Bush, 151

Fate and fortune, 22

Ferguson, Adam (father), 1-2, 3, 7, 9

Ferguson, Adam,
childhood, 1-3
death, 19
education, 3-7
family, 1-3, 12, 13, 18, 19
friendships, 4-5, 18, 72, 90-1, 92, 101
health, 17, 18
impact and influence, 14, 119-20
military career, 7-8, 9, 56, 105, 107, 110
politics, 2-3, 10-11, 16-17, 83, 85-88, 111, 113-14, 140, 139-41, 144-5
religious opinions, 2-3, 4-6, 10, 19
students and teaching, 14-15, 31, 34, 35, 40-1, 44, 110, 124

Ferguson, Sir Adam (son), 17

Ferguson, Katharine (wife), 13, 18

Fingal, 11

Flanders, 7, 18

Fletcher, Andrew, of Saltoun, 97-8, 99, 104, 105, 117, 131

Fletcher, John, 9

Florence,
Ferguson visits, 18
republican era, 96

Fontenoy, 7

Forbes, Duncan, judge and adminis-

trator, 51

Forbes, Duncan, historian, 153

France, 72, 114
Enlightenment, 47-8
Ferguson visits, 15
Renaissance, 43-4
Revolution, 17, 18, 52, 88, 101, 108
wars with Britain, 7-8, 10-11, 18, 88, 92, 105, 108

Gaelic and Gaels, 2, 5, 7, 8, 11-12, 56, 74, 149

Garve, Christian, 128, 129-30, 132

Gellner, Ernest, 145

Geneva, 15

Gentleman's Magazine, 121-2

George III, King of Great Britain, 92

Germany, 72, 78
ancient condition of, 66
Anglomanie, 132
Anglophilie, 128
Aufklärung, 128-31, 132, 133
Ferguson's influence in, 128-34, 142-3, 148, 152
Ferguson visits, 8, 15, 18

Gibbon, Edward, 92, 93, 127

Gillies, John, 106

Glasgow,
town and society, 80
University of, 3, 6, 21, 23-4, 25, 47, 48, 63, 73, 78, 122, 135

Gordon, Sir Robert, of Gordonstoun, 22

government, 43-4, 45-6, 62, 91, 94-9, 103, 110-17, 130

Gracchi family, 96

Graham, H.G., 18

Gramsci, Antonio, 145